ARCTURIAN STAR CHRONICLES

VOLUME ONE

Songs
OF THE
Arcturians

Dear Cindy! Richard
2 can barely begin
to express my gratitude to
you for bringing The dream
into book form. The Arcturians
told me you long years that 2
would find you when the
Time was right. 2 am
so grateful for everything.
Patricia Pereira

INTERGALACTIC
SEED MESSAGES FOR
THE PEOPLE OF PLANET EARTH

Songs
OF THE
Arcturians

A manual to aid in understanding
matters pertaining to
personal and planetary evolution

Patricia L. Pereira

BEYOND
WORDS
Publishing
I N C

Beyond Words Publishing, Inc.
4443 NE Airport Road
Hillsboro, Oregon 97124-6074
503-693-8700
1-800-284-9673

Design: Leigh Wells
Composition: Fay Bartels
Editor: Sue Mann
Proofreader: Marvin Moore

Printed in the United States of America
Distributed to the book trade by Publishers Group West

Library of Congress Cataloging-in-Publication Data

Pereira, Patricia L.
    Songs of the Arcturians : a manual to aid in
understanding matters pertaining to personal and planetary
evolution / Patricia L. Pereira.
        p.   cm. — (Arcturian star chronicles ; v. 1)
    "Intergalactic seed messages for the people of planet earth."
    ISBN 1-885223-43-9
    1. Human-alien encounters. 2. Telepathy. I. Title. II. Series:
Pereira, Patricia L.   Arcturian star chronicles ; v. 1.
BF2050.P47   1996
133.9'3—dc20   96-9875
                                                                  CIP

The corporate mission of Beyond Words Publishing, Inc.:
    Inspire to Integrity

Dedication

For Patrick and Sharon

Table of Contents

PART III

Essays from Arcturus

CHAPTER 1

CHAPTER 2

CHAPTER 3

CHAPTER 4

CHAPTER 5

CHAPTER 6

Personae

THE ARCTURIANS: Fifth- and sixth-dimensional beings of light from Blue Crystal Planet in the Arcturian star system (also called the Bootes system). The handle of the Big Dipper points directly to a bright star, which is Arcturus. One of the "jobs" of the Arcturian star council is to serve Spirit upon the Supreme Hierarchical Council for Planetary Ascension, System Sol. Base of operations: Saturn.

CRYSTALLINE LIGHT ESSENCE: Feminine energy from Arcturus. Name not translated, but means "musical note like the chiming of a glass bell."

PALPAE: Arcturian galactic envoy, Ambassador of Light, Love, and Peace, Intergalactic Brotherhood of Light, to people of planet Earth. Preparer and sealer of documents. Patricia's primary spiritual guardian. Masculine vibration.

QUAKER: Arcturian "seed planter." Greeter of newly established human telepaths. Door opener. Masculine vibration.

QUANTRA: Arcturian solar scientist. Guides and directs flows of energy that emerge from the radiance of the sun(s). Harmonizes webs of the stellar grid. Solar-body essence. Masculine vibration.

QUOARTS: Arcturian lunar scientist. Guides and directs flows of energy emitted by moons. Moon-body essence. Feminine vibration.

SANANDA: The Christ, or High Christ Consciousness. Christ Essence. Higher vibrational identification given to Earth's Avatar Supreme by the Intergalactic Brotherhood of Light. Incarnated upon Earth as Jesus, Krishna, Buddha, Mohammed, Quetzalcoatl, and more. Masculine vibration.

TASHABA: Catlike entity from the Sirian star system. Serves upon zoo, or ark ship. Gathers DNA and spirit essence of Earth's endangered and extinct species for future retrieval upon Earth or for return to stars of origin. Feminine vibration.

Introduction

I was forty-eight years old when I became aware that I am telepathically connected with extraterrestrials from the Arcturian star system. In retrospect, I remember a night when, as a child of seven or eight, I awoke to a crackling sound emanating from the basement of my home. Tiptoeing to the top of the stairway accompanied by our Doberman pinscher, I peered down at a light as bright as the noonday sun. The house appeared to be on fire. Instead of crying out to my parents, I just stood there with my quivering dog. I clearly remember calling out, "Who's there, who's there?" Then I went back to bed. I never spoke of the event until recently. As a young teenager in the early 1950s, I was walking home from church one star-tossed evening pleading with the night sky, "Come help us! Come help us!" I now know a part of me has always realized we are not alone.

I always had difficulty saying the word *God.* I felt embarrassed, ashamed. What I was taught by my church made God seem small, demanding, vindictive, and contracted. I decided that I must be an agnostic, perhaps even an atheist. Searching for mental, emotional, and spiritual satisfaction, I began to study world history and the philosophy of the Greeks, Germans, French, English, and Americans. Then, in the early 1980s, I was invited to a question-and-answer session with two very aware spiritual teachers, Sharon and Patrick O'Hara. Moments into the evening, all my doubts and frustrations slipped away. Instantly, my life changed. I began to meditate in earnest. Expanding my philosophical studies, I explored Native American spirituality, Buddhism, Hinduism, Taoism. Time with God and serving God became the primary focus of my life.

In the transformative year of 1987, the year of the Harmonic Convergence, I was a divorced medical transcriptionist who had become infatuated with the issue of reintroducing wolves into the Yellowstone ecosystem. A few years earlier, I had started an environmental educational organization in Boise, Idaho—the Wolf Recovery Foundation. Though busy with all the details of running the fledgling foundation, I set aside time each day to meditate upon spiritual matters. One sunny June morning, I happened upon a copy of *With Wings of Eagles* by John Randolph Price. He suggested that if one wants to channel, one simply sits quietly in meditation and records what comes. As I did so, I became immediately aware of word thoughts drifting lazily through my head that seemed different, but yet similar, to mine. I wrote word after word. When I was finished, I thought, What gibberish, what nonsense. A few days later, I read what I had written and discovered I had composed a poem, "Give Honor to Your Dark Side," which is in the beginning of this book.

I thought, This is pretty amazing, and I decided to give it another go. Instantly, I received the transmission "Greetings." I "heard" a happy, chuckling sound inside my head that identified itself as Quaker. I was puzzled; what was this? A few days later I experimented again and was introduced to Palpae. I was told that Palpae is an entity from Arcturus whose body is made up of light substance. Palpae is my main contact, my mentor, my constant, thought-connected companion. Soon I began to look upon Palpae as a wise, gentle, loving father figure.

Palpae and the Arcturians I communicate with hail from the fifth and sixth dimensions. The star Arcturus and her planets form a multidimensional solar system. To locate Arcturus in the night sky, find the Big Dipper. The handle points directly toward a large bright star. That shimmering star is Arcturus.

We who reside in the slower-vibrating third dimension experience our bodies and the world as physical matter. The fifth- and sixth-dimensional Arcturians, however, live upon planets that vibrate, not as physical matter, but as light. My understanding is that a dimension is like a musical octave. Earth vibrates slowly and is a heavier octave or dimension. As a planet begins to refine or quicken its vibration, it becomes lighter and lighter until, eventually, it moves up the scale into the adjoining octave or dimension. I am told that, in our universe, for every physical planet there are at least four or five light-substance planets.

Because of my increasing connection, I became interested in the phenomenon called channeling. I found that the well-known channels of the day—Knight, Pursel, and the like—are primarily trance channels. That is to say, consciousness leaves their bodies while entities speak through them. Others do automatic writing, their hands moving as if by themselves.

It seems to me that with the upgrading of energies upon the planet, channeling is evolving. Since 1987, I have met many people who are quite consciously aware that they are telepathically connected to spiritual beings from various dimensions. I believe that each of us, in our own unique, creative way, will one day be consciously connected with Spirit. One purpose of these collected writings is to assist you in unlocking the doors of your mind to the majestic spiritual worlds.

When I connect telepathically to other dimensions, I must always know where I am tapping into. Entities who reside in the lower domains of the fourth dimension (called the astral plane) can be quite manipulative and controlling. Twice in my early weeks I failed to "hook up" properly, and extraterrestrials commonly referred to as the Grays invaded my mind. The experience was upsetting and quite frightening. I quickly learned to check my sources. I discovered that certain words or phrases contain highly refined vibrations that cannot be used in telepathic communications by negative-oriented beings. Though not included in the written transcripts, the greeting "Hum of the many planets" or the salutation "Adonai" immediately assures me and identifies my level of connection.

In his initial transmission, Palpae stated, "Please understand that our language and yours are not synonymous. We will attempt to communicate with you in overtones that are equivalent to your personal perception of language." Many times I have had cause to reflect upon these lines. English is one of the most difficult languages for expressing spiritual concepts. For instance, the beings with whom I am in contact always refer to themselves as "I/We." It is the clearest way to describe an individual who is in constant harmonic communication with Cosmic Mind, That Which Is One. However, to make reading this book easier, I decided to use "I" when the being communicating refers to himself or herself, and "we" when the being refers to Arcturians or other galactic species in the collective.

The Arcturians use many descriptive terms to identify God. Their purpose is to expand our perception of God, the universe, and self as Soul (a spiritual being cloaked in a physical form). Additionally, they refer to Christed Energy as Sananda, or The Essence. Christ is defined by Paramahansa Yogananda in *Divine Romance* as one who "rose above ordinary human consciousness and entered the cosmic Christ Consciousness, the pure reflection of God present in all creation." The Arcturians recognize Christ Consciousness as one who has incarnated upon Earth many times to serve all humanity, not only as Jesus, but also as Krishna, Buddha, Lao Tsu, Moses, Mohammed, Quetzalcoatl, and The Dawn Star, among others.

The primary purpose of these essays is to acquaint you with principles of Universal Law and to introduce you to our brothers and sisters from the stars. The writings contain information to prepare us for galactic citizenship. The Arcturians remind us of our collective role as planetary stewards and of our responsibility to interact in a peaceful, loving, protective manner with all of Earth's life forms. They want to expand our perceptual horizons until the energy we now expend focuses upon our inner lives as Soul in service to Greater Good, or God.

In closing, I would like to devote a few moments to thank the people who have supported and encouraged me over the years to persevere, until 1994 when I connected with Cynthia Black and Richard Cohn, the visionary owners of Beyond Words Publishing, who courageously challenged themselves to publish this manuscript. In particular, I want to thank my spiritual sister Clare Heartsong; Barbara Eddy, for being my creative mentor and inspiration; Linda Erickson, for her early editing efforts; my husband, Clifton, for his loving steadfastness; my beloved spiritual teachers, Patrick and Sharon O'Hara; and special thanks to my editor, Sue Mann, for her attention to detail and perfectionism, and for preserving the integrity of the work.

Statement of Purpose
for Earth Visitation

ARCTURIAN CONTINGENT, INTERGALACTIC
BROTHERHOOD OF LIGHT

We, who are of the Arcturian contingent, Intergalactic Brotherhood of Light, announce our presence before humankind. Hear us, people of Earth, for we have come to acquaint you with the processes of planetary evolution. Our purpose is to invite you to the stars. Our purpose is to awaken you to the experience of God's living presence as the focal point of your daily lives. Our purpose is to guide you in unlocking and accessing the dormant functions of your minds.

Welcome us, for we are of your family. We have come to prepare you for the greatest event in Earth's history.

Within the realms of present-day scientific knowledge, there is little that concurs with our methods; however, know that Earth is in the midst of an evolutionary event: the transposition of her material body to that of the essence of Spirit. Note well that the procedures and ramifications involved in the transformative process are manifesting galaxywide as well as within your planetary home.

Within this manuscript we will endeavor, as simply as possible, to refocus the priorities of your lives.

There will come a number of entities onto these pages. The majority of us hail from the Arcturian planetary system, although among us many star complexes, galaxies, and even universes are represented. Our emissaries stand ready to greet you. Eventually, you will come to recognize us all, for you are our lost brothers and sisters.

We serve under the auspices of Earth's Spiritual Hierarchy.

Give Honor to Your Dark Side

Give Honor to your Dark Side.
Honor the reflection of self in the eyes of another.

Use this experience to walk a path of wisdom,
to grow,
to release your self-imposed
traditions of the past,
outmoded ways of acting,
of perceiving and believing.

All that you wish to be free of is inside the Self.
Look at these things.
Honor them for their gifts to you.
Then, let them fly from the wings of
your consciousness.

Let go. . . .
And thus,

Travel to the stars.

The Initial Song, June 1987

Prelude

Palpae, as part of the telepathic mind of the Arcturian galactic envoy to planet Earth, sends greetings. We have traveled over vast distances of interstellar space to salute our brothers and sisters of planet Earth. For many, many aeons, beings of light from the stars have observed your world, and the plains of Earth are rich in clues that speak of our presence.

Evolution's hour has arrived; the time is ripe for this generation of humans to awaken. In the early years of the coming century, the time for the starships' subtle maneuverings will end. The men and women of Earth will find themselves conspicuously introduced to beings of light of the Intergalactic Brotherhood and the coordinating councils that oversee your solar system's spatial quadrants.

As humans began to develop a taste for living in a state of obscure autonomy at a very critical juncture in their prehistory, they decided to reject even the slightest hint of interference in their private affairs by outside forces. It was at that time that the Memories, which their conscious minds once held of the worlds of light, became lost to all but a very few. Paradoxically, humans concurrently came to the conclusion that they had been left to fend for themselves. As the sorrow of loneliness overcame them, they became enmeshed in the webs of spiritual sleep.

As immature humans ventured forth to discover their new world, they gradually became consumed by and fascinated with their biological urges as well as intoxicated with the sweet taste of acquiring objects. As they became increasingly distracted by the majestic beauty of Earth and more delighted with the pleasures of the physical form, the Memories began to fade more rapidly. Because humans generally neglected things of the Spirit, the knowledge the ancient ones had openly shared with them in the years of innocence was withdrawn and buried until such time that the awakening ones began to mature.

In this introductory segment, I will explain how and why the person who has recorded these writings was chosen to consciously interact with the beings of light. This entity's—Patricia's—life has seen much struggle, and her pathway to the Memories has wound like a snake slowly making its way over rock-sharp terrain. If you correctly intuit your heart's emotional responses to the paragraphs of this narrative, your essence will begin to clearly comprehend the many ways you resemble this simple woman who found herself conscripted quite abruptly into the Arcturian galactic light forces to serve as a telepathic energy receptor and transmitter.

If you were to come upon Patricia, you would not easily recognize the power and heat that has been granted her to emanate; indeed, she herself is quite unaware of the depth of its magnitude. She is surrounded by many people who would never presume to consider her private activities, those moments when she makes herself available to the communicative thoughts of extraterrestrial beings. How could this woman have logically reasoned that one beautiful summer's day in her life's middle years, as she began to experiment with writing the softly forming words she heard drifting through the back of her mind, she would find herself startled by the presence of a telepathic energy laughingly calling himself Quaker? How could she know that this essence would shortly be replaced by the resonant vibrational hum of a being who Patricia would soon come to know as her special star guidance counselor, Palpae of Arcturus, who introduced his substance as a being whose purpose is to serve the people of planet Earth as an ambassador representing the multidimensional Intergalactic Brotherhood of Light?

Why, then, was Patricia contacted for this assignment, and not yourself?

Although it is true that the preparation of this manuscript is Patricia's challenge to perform, the talented gifts of all spiritually evolving humans are of great import in aiding aspects of planetary evolution. In fact, you are all encoded with a personal matrix of information that is poised, ready to activate the expression of purpose into your daily lives. Spinning and spiraling, the DNA helix impregnates the tissues and membranes of your bodies with genetic data that contain all your minds need to access the finer vibrating hum of the light worlds. Like threads caught up in Creation's robe, cords of pure light insinuate themselves into the emotional fibers of your hearts, assuring the eternal *you* integral positions in the cosmic design.

Purpose arises out of Love's perfect energy. Purpose unfulfilled is like a patiently smoldering ember. The spark of spiritual passion applied to the human intellect is the kindling that sets the flames of purpose blazing. One's inner fire then erupts as a burning desire to intimately serve God—the Omnipotent One.

The longing to fulfill one's higher purpose is an acute and chronic desire that permeates the core of a being who is serious about personal spiritual transformation. The awakening ones are among those who incorporate within their emotional fields an intense yearning to transcend the pervading ennui of third-dimensional spiritual sleep.

The transmissions from Patricia's pen incorporate within them certain energy themes whose patterns are especially designed as a series of primer informational packets. It is my pleasure to scatter symbolic word pictures before your eyes like seeds sown upon fertile ground.

To encourage the germination and maturing of humanity's return to innocence, and with the specific permission of the star councils, Patricia has been directed to modify, simplify, and clarify the solar-to-Earth data-disk transmissions that make up her manuscript within the limitations inherent in human communication. Therefore, this book is an experiment that transcends the idea of channel. These essays are a co-creative work. They are written by Patricia in close companionship with and in observational monitoring of all data by beings of light that counsel her.

Patricia's first consciously stated intention to commit her life in service to the Absolute took place several years prior to that afternoon in 1987 when she abruptly found herself face-to-face with extraterrestrials. While performing Tai Chi, which she believed capable of sustaining heightened energies within its yielding patterns, she clearly and somewhat forcefully transmitted her emotion-filled pledge and called upon That Which Is to assist her. Unaware that she had been born with the specialized talents peculiar to a high-velocity solar-star-connected telepath, the power of the transmissions issuing from her mind reverberated through the ethers like thunder following a bolt of lightning. Engulfed with an energy that flooded over her like waves coming from the sea while evoking her personal image of God to hear her, she dedicated her life to serve that which Spirit willed of her.

It was not long after this episode that Patricia suddenly found herself consumed with the desire to participate in bringing a healing upon a species of animal that resonated with the same hum as her beating heart: *Canis lupus*, the wolf. To this day, Patricia's intellectual self cannot rationally or logically explain to other humans the single-minded passion and unwavering determination that in midlife suddenly overtook and possessed her. Her almost instantaneous devotion to an animal she had never seen was so intense that it elicited a courage from her never before hers, a force so empowering she found it within her ordinarily shy and private self to stand before strangers to teach them and share with them the beauty and majesty of the animal. Not content to rest, she wrote reams of letters to many people and formed an organization so that others whose hearts smoldered with love for the elegant creature might come together to accomplish a mutual goal. Thus, this woman earned and was granted the right by the star tribes to use the title Manitu (spirit keeper) as if it were her name.

I have encouraged Patricia to share this aspect of her life's story to enable you to comprehend more clearly that within the regions of your hearts a great passion also lies buried. I would have you understand that the *you* who you are is an essential cog in Creation's wheel. The people who are fully cognizant of the magnitude of their human potential are few; for the majority, absolute self-knowledge lies hidden within the recesses of their hearts.

Seek! Seek that which is thy greater Self!

As a whole, humanity is in a state of great despair. The men, women, and children of your planet are quickly losing hope that they will ever make right that which most profoundly torments them. Although we do not suggest that you put aside all you possess to accomplish the highest purpose for which your particular self was fashioned, we do recommend that you closely observe the rituals of your daily life while you endeavor to enhance awareness of your higher Self until you are adept in interpreting its whispers. How magnificent it would be if all humans were to set aside a minimum of an hour each day to actively participate in some form of practical or ceremonial healing beneficial to themselves, their fellow beings, and Earth as well.

Are you one who has put your relationship with the Creator on the back burner of your life's interests, and do your personal disappointments and sorrows seem just too much to bear? No matter the predicaments of your life, deep within you carry an innate knowledge of the profound. There, hidden in the subconscious, you remember the universe.

Come. Learn to concentrate your energies. Endeavor to walk the sacred, spiritual path. Focus your mind and emotions upon Love's rhythms only and, in spite of yourself, you will begin to sparkle like a living rainbow. Surely then your day's load will become lighter. Remember, these are magical times!

Resolve to take your place among those who are earnestly and courageously working to ease the stress that, by necessity, accompanies a major shift in the polarities of a planet's vibratory hum. Become one with those who are the pioneers of the new dawn.

One cannot escape noticing the deterioration of human society, the rampant erosion and decay of the inner cities, and the grave ecological backlash resulting from overwhelming worldwide environmental pollution as well as ongoing massive deforestation. I will mirror our views to you as might a guest coming into your home whose eyes are greeted by a residue of dust and grease clinging to the surface of your finest crystal and china. Correspondingly, I will emphasize that as the awakening humans flow ever further into the energy fields of Love's radiant Oneness, they will inevitably begin to transpose the growing planetary wastes into a flowering mecca.

To merge with the higher vibrations that are the true influence behind planetary affairs, it is not necessary for you to be politically influential, to have great wealth, or to possess the noble stature of a renowned religious, political, or financial figure. You need not loudly reverberate like a boisterous strummer before whom young people swoon. As a consciously evolving being who is committed to spiritual Self-discovery, your inner light will naturally shine as brightly as a star. Earth, gentle, startled reader, is calling you. In the next years it will be the great unnoticed, those humans who are the fibers upon which society is hung, who will be the ones who are instrumental in precipitating massive cultural, environmental, and spiritual change.

So, how do you find your place and begin to transform a troubled world? Simply. Find a moment (and the courage and resolve as well) one day to telephone or write to your government's intrepid leaders. State clearly that you, as a citizen, petition them to demonstrate a greater regard for that which you cherish. Encourage them to serve their bewildered constituency in such a fashion that privately and publicly they will represent the highest ethical and moral ideals. Attend a gathering of like-minded people, those who share common problems or interests, who meet to embrace and comfort one another with words that elicit encouragement and love. Create an atmosphere of cheer and goodwill at your place of "busyness." When all is in chaos, laugh and smile and refrain from spilling the beans behind another's back. Become an island of peace in a sea of turmoil. Then, as night stretches her shadows, enclose the hands of your children within yours and remind them of their relationship with the angels. Do not let your children forget the knowledge of pure innocence that was theirs at birth.

The essays of this manuscript contain a multitude of

complex sentence structures; however, the basic intention behind the messages is quite simple: We would teach you to Love. We would have you experience Oneness as the natural state of your conscious being.

Additionally, we will represent ourselves in such a manner that the fright you normally experience when confronted with the realities of the "unknown" dissipates until it no longer holds fear's power over you. We are well aware that if a multitude of metallic-appearing starships were to suddenly materialize in the skies over your cities, such an event would serve no purpose but to startle and place fear's images before you.

Though this manuscript certainly is not our initial attempt to contact humanity, it has been compiled in such a manner as to awaken you consciously to our presence and to acquaint you further with the nature of our beings. We have found that the most beneficial method of announcing our intentions toward the species *Homo* is through the energies of creativity: music, film, paintings, literature, and the like.

People of Earth, you are our Oneness, you are our stellar family. You and we are not unlike a single cell in Creation's living body. May your loneliness slide comfortably away as you slowly realize that you are on the road to the stars.

What a sight, as we observe our awakening brothers and sisters and prepare your seats before the feasts of the universes!

The sparkling lights of the stars are calling you. Read further and come to know of us. These pages will acquaint you with beings of light who ride upon the starships. The essays will acquaint you with the sky warriors, or the eagles of the new dawn, our human and animal ground forces who are dedicating their lives to actively participate in the cosmic evolution of Earth, their planetary home. Among these beings are men and women very much like yourselves. In time, you will come to a complete understanding that the tie binding humanity to the stars is a linkage that has never really been broken.

As swallows fly on summer winds, you soar now, ever closer, on an unrelenting course whose destination is the stars.

This is our prelude. This is our song. A field conduit of light energy are we. Sweetly we sing for your delight.

Greetings

QUAKER

I am one who flows with the stars. I greet you from beyond your veil. Translucent and remarkable are your thoughts that shine before your world's image of night. Something tender transpires when your inner self feels complete, reflecting your soul like a light onto future's face.

Transfer the care of your being to God!

Heavy in the physical form, your human vibrations will benefit from the search alone, which must begin immediately, for the timing is urgent. Puddles of protein, humanity's slipping image of itself is radiating strain into the cosmos. Balance is needed. Know this: We prefer risk-takers. Will there be mushroom clouds or return of the "others"?

Early July 1987

Patricia Meets Palpae

PALPAE

Earth people, know that beings of light have descended in accordance with artifacts, such as the Pyramid of Giza and Stonehenge, anciently mapped upon your planet. Patricia, you have been blessed with a vision, a vision whose magnitude embraces the attainment of the stars. By willing to give up your life for your visionary dream, you are emanating catalytic energies. You and other humans like you serve as planetary light forces. The energies manifested by your dedication are essential to our purpose as we proportionally increase Earth's energies on a scale that cannot yet be imagined.

Your planet is calibrating celestial resonating periods. That is to say, its vibrational third-dimensional density state is being transplanted by fourth- and fifth-density restructuring in accordance with harmonics that are sung by the universe.

I speak to you from cloud tunes of the red sun. Promptly upon humans receiving this message, various sun alterations will occur on a level unseen by the sleeping people of Earth. These alterations are in preparation for solar events to facilitate interplanetary healing methods.

Fingers of cold liquid hydrogen radiating into space enable us to anticipate levels of chronic hypersensitivity. Humans who reflect the clarity of the Light-Love essence are essential to our purposes in maintaining global stability.

We of the stars beckon you. Our whispers reach into your hearts and into your dreams. In the light of Earth's new dawn, we dance among the awakening images of your slumbering minds.

Patricia challenged me: "Are you spiritual beings?"

YES! The harmonic frequencies of the universe allow us to radiate the beams of our essences toward humans only in accordance with God's plan, which is what humans term unconditional Love.

My name is Palpae. I am what you would recognize as a global statesman. Please understand that our language and yours are not synonymous. We will attempt to communicate with you in overtones that are equivalent to your perception of language.

Surrender Your Grief

Humankind . . .

Your answer is to surrender your grief.

The echoes of time bring this truth to you for the
   advancement of your soul.

Do not be fooled by the conscious mind that seeks complex answers to that which, in reality, is simplistic. Your
dedication to evolution has subjected you to the whims of
the material form.

Split fragments of self, you were divided by a veil of
thought. Traveler, yearn to be taught! The star dance will
fuse your soul.

In time you were severed. Wandering and seeking for
unrecalled millennia, you have united with other searching beings. You have gathered a coalition of souls about
you who are also seeking individually among the planes
of Earth. Together, yet you remain separate.

Some will pass through and
Some will choose to stay.
Focus your eyes on the suns of the many planets.
You travel through time and through you,
I Embrace the Universe.

You will see the many fires of the past
on the journey that leads to the Light.
All steps in the growth process that
leads to God Oneness.

The Second Song, June 1987

Song to the Earth

THE ARCTURIANS

Greetings to Earth from the starship *Marigold–City of Lights.*

We greet you at the dawn of your teeming glory.
Look, Earth people, to your
    ancestors from the stars.
God's Light dances in the ethers that
    surround your material beauty.
Tomorrow's fortunes present
    this truth to your reality.
The lights that touch you as you
    lean toward these sounds
Present themselves to you from the
    depths of your yearning minds,
Partially smothering the tears of
    your misunderstandings.

We invite you to look to the night
    for your answers.
Robed in starlight, our love envelops
    Our awakening children.

August 1987, retreat on the Yellowstone River

Chapter 1

STARSEED SEGMENTS

PALPAE

I would speak to those humans who have the idea that the grass is greener on the other side. I would have you become aware of the status of the beings who dwell upon starships. We live here, you see, as if enclosed in giant cocoons, wrapped and protected within the membranous shells of our ships. The starships themselves are essences of life, true miniaturized planets. Vibrancy surrounds us as our traveling dance moves us along the space grids, though in a very real sense the experience is not as openly free as it was when, bodies unencumbered, Patricia's willing eyes permitted our Onenesses to walk with her as she wandered among the trees and meadows of the sacred lands of the Yellowstone of the spirit gods and as she sat contemplating the grandeur of the Teton Mountains.

Do not wish yourselves upon us before you are ready, Earth people, you who are of so much latent beauty and talent. But many of you begin to sparkle, you see, sparkle and snap! The fidgeting of awakening is overtaking you. For our part, we have the good sense to know that it will take a certain quantity of "time," and so we sigh and comfort ourselves as we continue to await the spiritual rebirthing of Earth's evolving men and women.

Understand that our time, that which you describe as a time frame, is not the same for us as it is for you. Time is not a quantitative or qualitative thing that we hold closely and attempt to examine. That which you label time is nothing more than the pulsing ebb and flow of Creation's ever-expanding energies.

Although it is true that many of you will eventually join our Onenesses in service to the Absolute and you will be stationed with us upon the great starships, that moment is yet to come. While you wait, take every opportunity to bask in the pure, joyous sensations that physical life offers. Freely explore Earth's bounteous lands and seas. Revel in the vast distances and brilliant colors that abound in her skies.

Earth is in the midst of a quantum event. The radical quickening, or speeding up, of time is but one aspect of the ethereal adjustments being made in preparation for a massive spatial transfer of the planet and her inhabitants. These maneuvers, however, are not always noticeable to ordinary humans.

These are evolutionary times. An alertness of heart and mind will become a necessary state of being for the spiritually adventurous. Nevertheless, in future times you will look back upon these difficult years and give a nodding of head in solemn agreement to that which is written. You shall see.

Potentially destructive energies originate in men and women whose ego-inflated superiority ascribes themselves as "privileged" to possess the bulk of the world's wealth or position with the supposition (within their minds) that others are of lesser stature than their exaltednesses. Subsequently, writings of all Earth civilizations are replete with stories of generalized carnage and wholesale suffering. Throughout history, the actions of a handful of evil-minded people have punctured the peace and well-being of the majority of the inhabitants of your cosmically immature world. The Law of One has been twisted and manipulated. The reality of coexisting light worlds is deemed illusion. The accepted "norm" upon which human society is built is that human law is separate from cosmic law.

To otherwise enlighten: Our mother starship (symbolically named *Marigold—City of Lights* throughout these writings) is much grander in scope than you may imagine. However, her specific dimensions will not be clearly stated in these introductory chapters.

For your further edification, that which the Western world recognizes as Christ Essence, as "He who brings Love's energy," is One whom we serve and know by the name Sananda. Sananda is *the* chief creative energy for your spatial quadrant. In a variety of forms—Jesus, Buddha, Mohammed, for example—and in many places He has taken physical form to serve the diverse spiritual needs of the entire human family. When you limit recognition to an exterior body called Jesus as being the only Christ Essence, you discount His gift to all people and fail to recognize the truth of His teachings. His greater being is readily identifiable by His Love vibration and the purity of His light-field radiance.

Multitudes of words have been placed upon parchment to document what humans traditionally view as the wisdom of a variety of spiritual masters. To their misfortune, humans began preaching to themselves through a variety of complex doctrines, although their only need was to learn but one lesson: that of Love perfected within the Law of One. It needed no writing down. Those who implement the Law of One in physical life practice compassionate, unconditional Love for all God's creatures, including self. They live life to its fullest. Their profound capacity to love serves to the greater good of all beings, of all forms of light and material matter, no matter their spatial placement.

Unfortunately, it is a difficult thing for the ego to accept the reality of extraterrestrial, multidimensional worlds, a concept that fails to pass the ego's grand plan to test, touch, taste, feel, place in a box, analyze, pontificate upon, qualitate, and quantitate ad infinitum. Humans make quite ponderous and complicated what is meant to be utterly simple. In so doing, humans throughout history have been denied the role of active participants in inter-galactic affairs. However, we have always monitored and observed them.

Now a quorum of light-exuding men and women has elected to strive for spiritual maturity. Critically essential for transformation from the physical to the light body is to learn to Love, without expansion of ego, all creatures who call planet Earth home. As you begin to understand, you will start experiencing the underlying Oneness that embraces all things.

We address these matters for your august considera-tion. We are most anxious to have you return to cognizant interaction with your extrasolar family. Now that your electronic communication systems are being finely honed, we are able to reach larger numbers of you with ever-expanding degrees of information. You might, how-ever, waste less energy pointing radio antennae toward the stars. We have answered your signals: observe Patricia and the many humans with whom we have made con-scious, telepathic contact.

We realize that many of our writings will appear quite solemn, although Patricia has invited us to shake and rattle you as much as possible. Our mutual purpose is to awaken that which slumbers within you in comalike silence.

We urge you to closely observe your daily habits. Patricia recognizes that even with her awareness of the state of the Planetary Mother, she cannot help but over-step her own teachings. To honor the Law of Non-judgment is a difficult thing for her, for she loves wolves as the heart of her heart. She has not yet advanced to the point where she can be nonjudgmental with those who would kill or who would render other creatures without life or place to inhabit. As she considers such things, a great sadness and passionate fury rise within her. Much frustration comes to all of you who love Earth's natural grandeur and who, by necessity, must stand aside as you witness the ripping and tearing of Mother Earth's magnificent body by people who have little or no concern for the damage they inflict.

Patricia is aware, as she drives her car and uses other planetary resources, that she, too, plays a part in damaging the environment. She has not yet discovered how she might otherwise live in a metropolitan society. At this time, it is not possible. One cannot walk the streets and avoid breathing in and pushing out foul gases. One cannot avoid swallowing tainted water or ingesting toxin-containing foods. One cannot even travel safely from one point to another.

But those whom you consider as enemies one to another and that which is hoarded by the few by sapping the energies of the many are to become as naught in the years to come.

It is for finer minds than our Patricia's to work out solutions to the quandary that you have, in truth, brought upon yourselves. The world's governing bodies must begin, in a coordinated, voluntary effort, to find such solutions.

Humankind, you must accomplish these things with your free will shining forth. Those who choose otherwise, those who opt for status quo, will find themselves removed to a dark place resembling the sludge of sea-bottom mud. These things each of you must decide for yourselves.

I who prepare this telepathic relay hail from the great red sun of Arcturus. I am a galactic representative to Earth from the great star councils. I am in mind agreement with that of Omnipotent Light, fifth- and sixth-vibrational extraterrestrial beings in service to the Spiritual Hierarchy and our Lord Sananda. I state this for your life's pleasure to enhance.

Adonai.

On Time, Starships, Crystals, and the Awakening Earth

PALPAE

Time is an artificial enhancement of your created reality, and time is fading. Factors held to be within the realms of plausibility also have begun to fade. The people of Earth have embarked upon a great adventure. Evolutionary alterations underway are on a grander scale than even the most gifted mystics envision.

Step into the night with newly discovered wonder (those of you who come to wonder easily), for many ethereal beings flow around you and are subtly ripping the remnants of the veil that once securely divided the realms of spirit from the realms of the physical.

Planet Earth has entered an extremely critical phase in her spiritual evolution. Ponderous energies, birthed in humanity's negative thoughts, can no longer be contained as they radiate toxic poisons onto the space cords. In an effort to offset the resultant disharmony, we who hover gather before you for the purpose of radiating Light-Love energies earthward. To minimize physical stress upon your planet's body, we circulate currents of purified energy through you and through Earth and then, full circle, return them to merge with ours. We use rays of humming, rainbow-hued lights to perpetually cleanse residue of deleterious, outward-bound thought off the delicate space grids. Therefore, negative-charged particles are transformed into positive-charged particles prior to their release into the spatial star fields.

The illusive nature of your world can be spirit-shattering. Many are beginning to realize that what they have expanded their vital forces upon is, after all, only a mirrored silhouette of a greater reality. The majority of you are in dire need of spiritual nourishment to reinvigorate your emotional, mental, and physical harmony. Because of generalized soul hunger, your interpersonal relationships are no longer capable of fulfilling your most basic needs, an escalating condition that threatens to devour the weakened foundations upon which the institutions of your traditional society are built. As you struggle to discover and fulfill your cosmic destiny in accordance with that which has been foretold, an internal rift threatens to part your psyches.

Evolutionary times are holy times. In the not-too-distant future the forces of darkness that have enveloped the lands with their evil intent will be completely eradicated.

The perpetual conflict between good and evil will be no more. Many are already coming to an understanding that what they have always perceived as malevolent is, after all, only a warped expression of universal energy.

Your long-standing arrogant attitude toward Earth Mother is about to knock you humbly to your knees. However, you who awaken are arriving at an awareness that a good dose of gentle humbleness mixed with a splash of enlightened humility is mentally and emotionally rejuvenating and naturally strengthens your bodies' cells. The beauty of childlike innocence rests in you who develop a clear understanding of humility's humble song. You who humbly perceive Earth in her full magnificence truly understand the power of Love. Unwittingly, however, others have thrust themselves into a state of so-called humility that discourages the exercise of their powerful, latent potential and—behold the wonder—generally accepts the inevitable results as the grand plan. Too sad, too sad.

Many are becoming aware that the culturally fashionable quality you call time has begun to uncommonly quicken. From morn to dusk there is barely a breath of a moment to stop and take notice. The need for clocks is beginning to lessen. For millennia your souls have slumbered upon rafts of linear time as you drifted through the endless seas of third-dimensional sleep. Suddenly, you are being shaken awake, propelled by waves of escalating energy that are moving Earth and her inhabitants into position for a massive vibrational shift.

As fifth- and sixth-dimensional starships accelerate through layers of oxygen and other related gases that are life-giving breath to Earth, you may observe clouds that most eloquently outline them. This is particularly true in major cities for individuals who are beginning to awaken to their soul connection to the legions of Light. For their emotional comfort, we often prepare a personal salute by manifesting a series of cloud-formed starships. Gradually, more and more people are beginning to recognize when "UFOs" are cloaked in banks of wispy layered clouds.

Many of you have become entranced with the energies that crystals emit. We tell you that many crystals were purposely implanted within Earth to await that exciting moment when their specialized enticements would shine into your eyes. Then, intuitively entranced and with the ancient Memories stirring, you would be moved to take your preprogrammed crystal into your pocket or otherwise hang it securely about your person. After you secure it, the crystal will begin to radiate specialized light-encoded information, its assignment being to surround and cleanse your auric field so that you may more easily access the subtler, harmonic octaves.

Data contained in the above paragraph were transmitted via a light essence situated upon the sweet, sparkling beauty of the Blue Crystal Planet in the

Arcturian star system. Please be advised of this wonder. This message is of a particularly refined hum, and it is not an easy task for Manitu to fashion my thoughts. Therefore, this communique passes through the resonant mind of Palpae, whose vibrational pitch is more in keeping with that of the telepathic scribe-writer.

Crystals energized by the power of group thought are mechanisms that enable the propulsion of what humans perceive as flying saucers, but are, in fact, spinning miniaturized planets. Clear evidence of ether-bending, fifth- and sixth-dimensional starships will not be detected by your governments' measuring devices. Unfortunately, science continues to acknowledge the validity of "phenomena" that can be explained only within the narrow range of third-dimensional spatial graphs and measuring instruments. However, it behooves us to warn you, as gently as possible, that a great many, but certainly not all, sightings of UFOs are of marauding space rebels and do not represent the worlds of Light. If it so pleases you, we suggest that you carefully consider the foregoing.

I restate our position toward humankind as the same love and devotion as one extends to one's beloved family. Many critical events will take place in the coming years. To facilitate the transposition of Earth through the fourth and into the fifth dimension, it will, undoubtedly, be necessary to transmit many words spoken as parents with little time to teach their children many difficult lessons, when the parents know full well the dangers they must soon face. So it is, like watchful guardians we serve to the soul-safety of our (re)awakening children of planet Earth.

As you evolve, you will become aware of the multi-dimensional effects of thought and action. No longer will you perceive "reality" as a series of inflexible, time-static events. Most of you are more or less conscious of the "past." Some are even wise enough to see into the "future," if only from a trendsetting eye. In ancient times, stagnating forces imprisoned you by constricting your movements through a subtle manipulation of the time-space fabric. Suddenly, you found yourselves thrust out of Eden and into a state of perpetual unrest, a pivotal event that allowed a patriarchal-oriented point of view to sub-jugate you by convincing you of your inability to over-come your cosmic fate.

We boldly further state: The garden called Eden is not extinct. Its magnificence swirls all around you. Indeed, is Earth not a most beautiful jewel? You stepped out of the gate of your precious natal home when, in your heart-mind, you accepted fear as life's primary truth. At the moment you surrendered the power of unconditional Love as your one and only motivator, you succumbed to the forces of darkness. In the process you simply forgot that pure Love's innocence has always connected your heart-mind to the angelic realms.

It is time for spiritual courage, the courage to boldly search for that which you, as individuals and as a species, lost.

In the eyes of extraterrestrial beings of light who

reside upon starships, our brothers and sisters of Earth are, in essence, equal one to another and to us as well. The limitations you subject yourselves to rest in your illusory perception that one human is of considerable stature or of lesser stature than another. As if your collective mind were embedded in cement, you have surely allowed yourselves to be placed in servitude to the Dark Lords—evil, satanic beings who have manipulated humans throughout history—by accepting the spiritually defeating practice of "I'm superior, you're inferior" and "I'm inferior, you're superior."

From the ethers of the fifth- and sixth-dimensional hum these words transmit. I apprise you further that you will come to know joy's essence as a natural state of being. My praise is extended to those who are accepting of the wonders contained within the structures of this manuscript.

Adonai.

PALPAE

Patricia, we would appreciate your kind willingness to begin a project in affiliation with that of our own, if it so pleases you. We want to elevate the energy patterns of your people, for they suffer greatly and their sorrows run deep. That which is within them that seeks lives of honor, peace, and joy is, instead, laced with the resonations of mental, emotional, physical, and spiritual pain. We therefore request that you fully convey through the pages of this manuscript the essence of greetings and salutations that we, beings of light in residence upon *Marigold–City of Lights* and the many starships of the Intergalactic Brotherhood, extend freely to you. We have gathered our ships like the petals of a magnificent flower to surround your planetary system with the vibrations of universal Love and harmony.

In time, beloved among us, you will behold things

that will overwhelm your human senses of sight and hearing. Your voices, one day, will freely proclaim the wonders of the many marvels that have shown themselves to you. We have come to assist human and planetary evolution. However, for us to fully serve your larger needs, you must appropriately regard the essence of our spirits. It is for you to come to an understanding that we, who are miracles of God's creation, are no more or less than you are.

Of equal importance: In your role of planetary caretaker, you will be urged to elevate your level of appreciation for and association with other life forms inhabiting Earth. The entire spectrum of Earth's flora and fauna are held in Oneness within the intergalactic family, and thus are they as well in God's bounteous house. Therefore, be honorable before the presence of butterflies and moths, before the weeds and grasses that grow in rocky places. Consider well, consider well. And in so doing, you will become amazed as you develop a naturally rich and clear understanding of the purpose for life itself.

Radiate joyful thoughts consciously. Beam loving and peaceful images purposefully toward your planet, the dry plains of the moon, and the burning brilliance of the sun; then go deeper still until you have touched the mysterious star systems that wink at you from the night skies. The power of Love's harmony, when sung by your heart core in an innocent and sincere manner, radiates beams of light into the cosmos. In times of loneliness and sorrow, ponder this. It is not that we have forgotten you, it is that you have forgotten us.

We are the light of stars and the hum of distant planets. In the light of God's Love we journey upon our way. Do you suppose, therefore, that perhaps you are less than we? We reiterate: We are all One!

Every human carries qualities within that we term life's greater purpose or celestial activating task(s). Your primary task, when you find yourself caught up in the third-dimensional memory-restrictive plane, is to diligently search for that which you truly are. By embarking upon the path that leads to Self-discovery, you, too, will serve the resonant vibrational hum that is indicative of your soul's higher purpose. As you (re)discover the vastness that is the makeup of your soul's history, you will undoubtedly be most astounded. Yes, you most certainly will be amazed. As you seek to be one with the stars, you will begin to radiate upon the third-dimensional plane the native light that is the makeup of your greater Self.

On Humanity's "Negative" Nature, War, and Collective Suicide

PALPAE

We are of the opinion that many of the tunes we play may not be totally acceptable to your nature. Your prevailing disposition is to compromise knowledge by placing restrictive limitations upon information as it is transferred to your brain so that the results are more in keeping with your rigid, preestablished thought processes. Fortunately, slumbering near the surface of all but the most life-hardened, a delightful child roams freely within your heart-mind. This small being you once were patiently awaits an opportunity to emerge and shed light upon your forgotten dreams. It would be well to make an effort to rediscover what this innocent side of self was once about.

On this day, which is not so different from other days, the news is full of many woe-filled stories. We do not clearly understand why or how humans can be as cruel as they are, one to another. Your tendency is to dispense the energies of your inner fires through the violence of war, the turbulence of aggressive crimes, and all kinds of abuse upon the physical and emotional bodies of others. These fear-based forms of releasing energy, however, will no longer be even quasi-condoned as humanity moves into the dawn days of a more enlightened society. Firm notice is hereby given that those who have no sense of moral or ethical integrity in accordance with Universal Law, those who dissipate their energies in destructive acts, will not find themselves inhabiting this world in the future.

These dreadful occurrences, however, have been foretold and should not be a surprise. The acceleration of traumatic events worldwide and the rapidly escalating state of electronic technology that encourages simultaneous and minute observation by the masses actually facilitate the releasing of cloistered pockets of negativism that penetrate the planetary skin. Like pustules arising upon a diseased body, the pestilent energies of the Dark Lords will continue to fester and erupt as long as humanity continues to passionately court its prevailing mistress: that vixen, fear.

Fortunately, people who emit emotional patterns that arise from Love's powerful force temper and moderate your planet's bodily stressors. But the people who remain enamored with the ways of violence as they embrace death will be placed in a holding area until their spirit essences are reassigned forms in a harmonic density similar to Earth's present state. Or perhaps they will find themselves in the dark shadows of even heavier tones.

The Spiritual Hierarchy cooperates with Soul to manipulate each spirit into a particular body before a new life is to begin. However, this task is not carried out as punishment for sinful transgressions as defined by the religiously dogmatic.

To illustrate: If a child is to fulfill the qualifications necessary to graduate from grade to grade in your educational system, he or she must first execute a set number of assignments and tests to the satisfaction of the teacher, or face being retained at the same grade level for another period of time, or even, in some cases, face demotion to a lower learning level. Similarly, by completing certain predetermined criteria in life, one's spirit progresses through successively finer vibratory fields until, eventually, the soul passes into God's palace, the Temple of Peace. It continuously refines itself over a vast period of time until it shines in brilliant unison and with the same purity that marks the exquisitely etched lights of the spiritual realms.

Eventually, humanity's sores will be completely lanced and all disagreeable purulence purged from its societies, for to tokenly treat humanity's cancerous wounds would not cause a permanent remission of that which is a chronic and potentially mortal disease.

You who reach out to embrace the greater human family in order to share with them the wonders of the spiritual experience cannot bring yourselves to turn your backs coldly upon your people; they are like your flesh and blood, though with the cries of the tormented they incessantly wage war and commit rape and pillage upon one another. Do not cause yourselves undue dismay for the welfare of those unfortunate beings, for eventually their darkened spirits will turn from their downward path and they, too, will search for the light of God. It is well to recall the false pride you once carried and the prick of a vigilant awareness that brought you to the point of consciously noticing the brilliance of impending awakening.

Varying degrees of darkness exist within all humans, for the state of being human holds within it, at the very least, a minute fragment of tawdry thoughts that hovers around your emotions, awaiting its moment to lessen the beauty of your lives, no matter how closely you monitor yourselves.

The disharmonizing tones of human history have essentially predicated humanity's eventual demise. If you closely inspect your history as recorded in the books of Memories, you cannot escape observing your propensity to destroy that which you have created. Humans seem perpetually bent in an attitude that renders them incapable of escaping from their chronic fondness for the games of war. Though their methods of approaching battle have shown little real variation over the millennia, certainly the design and execution of weapons have escalated alarmingly. They now not only contemplate nuclear annihilation but have devised the means to effectively achieve it. Absurdly, humans seem to almost welcome the idea of inevitable collective suicide.

Like spoiled children, from generation to generation the people of your planet have ranted and raved at one another. From aeon to aeon, the destructive energies of ceaseless combat have swarmed about your battered globe; only the faces of the players have changed. But have they? Perhaps, after all, the spirit-selves of your beings are the same and only your bodies have altered their forms. Effectively, you are the same dancers dancing the same dance over and over to the tune of one interminable song.

The time has arrived when you are to put aside your childish toys, for you are to advance to a state of planetary maturity. However, to sweep away the accumulated dust of centuries, you will need to closely reexamine the pride you feel in your mastery and accomplishments in the "art" of war.

Adieu. In Oneness with all matter is Palpae. I salute the efforts of the awakening humans who faithfully and trustingly uplift their faces to receive the warming touch that is the breath of God.

TASHABA

Gentle friends, I would persuade you to heed my words. Patricia has spent her evening talking to young people who have been physically or emotionally abused by members of their own blood families. She had been invited to describe to these unfortunate children the misfortunes and sufferings of the wolf animal; she has returned home in a state of emotional distress from the sadness of their stories.

As a whole, the young people of your planet have become disenchanted, and the future looms before them, black and uninviting. The rigidity of the "ruling," decision-making adults is disruptive to the rhythms of their hormonal flows. The purity of their innate essences is easily disturbed by rays of negativity emitted by the bitter, emotional energies of their elders. As adolescents advance into the years of teenagehood, as they enter into the final stages of third-dimensional planetary sleep, the wisdom of the Soul recedes ever deeper into their sub-conscious regions. They are at an age when the final flut-tering occurs before they stretch forth into the spiritually comalike years of human "maturity."

As your spirit was born into your form of a human infant, it consciously retained its ancient Memories. But while you took your first breath, the vibratory essences humanity constantly emits began to seductively demolish the ability of your brain to retain them. One insidious step after another was taken throughout your infancy and childhood as you succumbed to the energies that inhabit your spiritually inattentive world. Then, in the years when the bloom of adolescent youth was upon you, the battle that waged inside you to recover your dissolving Memories was offset by the shooting pangs of undesirable and progressive somnolence. In the resulting fumbling, the Memories were permanently and effectively shoved into an uncomfortable place that humanity has labeled "only your imagination."

Youths' great love for far-out movies is a clue parents often miss of children's desires to retain their sanity in a totally confused world full of emotional and intellectual discordance. Youths' preferred music also is a stomping upon the elder-approved "norm," but by the very nature of its harsh abrasiveness, this music is self-defeating and carries them ever further down the very pathway they have vainly struggled to avoid.

As the times progress into the era of the golden dawn,

your moments of memory retention will lengthen until, finally, as the great day arrives when collective humanity is invited to take its place as a functioning member of the great star councils, your soul Memories will be recalled from all the years of your many lives. The veil that separates you from worlds of subtler vibrations will completely dissolve, and the people of your planet will truly come to know the glorious ecstasy that is life lived in God Oneness.

Some of the awakening believe that they have already achieved a state of spiritual bliss, that they perpetually reside in the absorbing hums of universal goodness. It is true that in moments of sublime stillness the human heart-mind may sufficiently quiet long enough to focus attention upon the profound majesty of Omnipotent Presence. However, it is not possible for a being encased in a third-dimensional body to ceaselessly uplift itself into a refined state in which unconditional Love and peace become a sum total experience. Furthermore, gentle brethren who hunger so for the stars, though you may quite beautifully exclaim that "to know Self is to know God," I must state that until you are able to fully comprehend and clearly recognize every step your soul has taken from the beginning through all the many cycles and rhythms of a multitude of physical manifestations, you know God but a fraction, just as you know Self but a fraction. One cannot state "I know Self a little" and pronounce such a remark as absolute.

Throughout these essays we outline many subjects for

your worthy consideration. As you ponder them closely you should ascertain that, although we have written a multitude of words, theme variations are simply constructed. There will come a time when you will lay aside your love of complexity for the wonders of brevity, such as when you master the art of moonbeam gathering. Ponder ye on how such a delight is to be accomplished? We will be greatly joyed to share the knowledge of many marvelous things with you, but first you must be willing to unconditionally embark upon the search for your soul's true residence, your spiritual Home, the great chamber of the Central Sun.

PALPAE

The final outcome of star-to-Earth directional motivators is predicated upon your understanding that human involvement is necessary. A quorum of your positive thought energies will expand the tones of Earth's natural vibrational hum. As you become spiritually active, you will participate with us to ease Earth into position to gently accept the rapidly accelerating transgalactic rhythms.

Hundreds of thousands of galactic beings live on Earth as humans. This is not to imply that all Earth-based life originated upon planets that swirl about distant stars. Assuredly, it did not. However, living upon Earth in human as well as other form are those who wander, which will be further explained.

This information is to enhance your understanding of who you really are. It is not a lesser or grander thing to be from either here or there. Placement is predicated upon what is most appropriate for your soul's level of spiritual awareness and self-willed traveling plan for third-dimensional lessons in becoming One.

If it pleases you, methods to activate your prelife—your encoded memory chips—will continue to awaken you in a continuous, escalating manner. We are of the opinion that those who have diligently read thus far, having paid careful attention to the details, will have decided to either accept or reject the authenticity of the writings. Therefore, we will concentrate our energies to serve those who hold faith in the truth of that which confronts them. We shall call upon those less agreeable another day, when they have become more favorably attuned to the believability of such grave matters as are herein contained.

Significant breakthroughs in our endeavors to contact you are beginning to emerge as more and more people awaken to the nature of their relationships with intergalactic beings of light. That which was foreseen progresses. However, many questions arise in the minds of those who have not yet found that for which they seek. The answer to the many questions that fling out from the depths of their yearning minds is *One!*

The foregoing is a summation statement, for it completely answers all your questions. We encourage you to look inward, deep into the chambers of your heart's greatest passion, to make acquaintance with your personal linkage to star-originating data. As you continue your journey of Self-discovery, you will see that thought-to-thought connection does provide.

Multidimensional Earth

Palpae

Bright orbs of a million or more stars, swirling as one
majestic galaxy, drift dreamily through space until, eventually, they reach the autonomous realms where one universe blends with that of its adjoining celestial neighbor.
Quasars are regions where a particular universe expands
its symphonic chorus to harmonically blend with that of
the zones of tranquility where spatial edge melds with
spatial edge, and so on and so on without limitation. What
we ineptly describe as a universal termination point has,
in cosmic reality, no beginning, no middle, no point
of absolute ending. We cannot adequately explain in
English what is limitless. The human mind does not easily
comprehend outside the sensory-field range of third-
dimensional reality; to date, Earth science completely
fails to acknowledge the possibility of multilayered dimensions of life within the planets of its own sun system.

There are many things that exist right under your noses, yet for the most part you choose to ignore them, even with a multitude of microscopes and telescopes with which to snoop and poke about. As an example, Earth's astral or etheric regions (the fourth dimension) remain unseen and untouchable. However, shamans from certain "uncivilized" societies have always moved in and out of the astral at will.

As material-manipulating technology developed and militarily and economically strong nations became dedicated to controlling the affairs of "less fortunate" people, the challenge of exploring alternative worlds lost its fascination. Third-dimensional physical-plane reality became much more real, much more immediate. In spite of the difficulties involved, however, a small segment of humanity for whom the Memories remain sacred, through the power of self-determination, has learned to focus its thoughts on that which is sight unseen and hearing unheard.

We know that many who read this manuscript will do so because they have embarked upon a great adventure. You are ones who search for greater meaning. You yearn to discover higher purpose, to connect with higher Self, to experience Oneness with God. Hope swells delicately within your breasts, like the fluttering wings of a small bird. A sense of the profound expands within your hearts. You are the ones who dare fly above the stark despair that envelops Earth. Like unto eagles are you!

That which we write as *Is*, is attainable. Remember, your thoughts will manifest future's reality.

Introduction to the Sun
and the Solar Language

QUANTRA

The inner lights of awakened humans shine like the brightest stars. Yet for thousands of years you have been unwilling to tap into the awesome power of your latent psychic abilities. Instead, you have preferred grubbing about the land with your focus primarily directed upon the dubious pleasures of various sensual enchantments. Secretly, you fear a realization of destiny manifested. You are equally terrified of becoming the recipient of disapproving, scornful contempt from your peers. But in this regard, history as humanity has fashioned it is coming to an end.

All over the world, thousands of courageous men and women are feeling compelled to throw off the dark cloaks of self-doubt and self-defeat. Endeavoring to awaken spiritually, they yearn to receive what is, after all, their right: access to the vast array of their full, dormant potential.

They are passionately drawn to gratifying their goals as if they were being summoned to self-fulfillment by the magnetic rays of a beckoning sun.

Indeed, a sun is much more than a flaming ball of hydrogen showering heat and light upon its planetary children. As the first evidence of God in manifest expression, a sun serves its familial solar system primarily as a depository for celestial knowledge. A sun's core could be likened to a gigantic cosmic library whose contents patiently await plucking, like ripened grapes hanging from a vine.

Rightfully, you may query, "How is one such as myself to partake of this sumptuous feast?" "Simply," we say. In utter stillness all that God Is and all that God radiates is yours to use. Meditate upon the sun. Setting all expectations aside, allow your imagination to blend your brilliant inner self with the warmth of Earth's sun. Submerge yourself into the sun's magnificent luminescence as if you were floating, caressed by the gentlest of waters. Contemplate upon the images that arise from deep within you. Harmonize and balance your powerful emotions until you and your sun-father become as One.

Though, now and then, life's sorrows and anxieties may leave you feeling emotionally or physically depleted, at all times your parent sun is ready and available to receive your transmitted thoughts. The sun's blazing fire contains all the comforts of greater Home revisited. As the times of the forward years wrap Planet Mother in their soft embrace, the thoughts and emotions of a peace-filled people will spontaneously and automatically drift to the sun as they seek to harvest the fruits of higher knowledge, that which is the lawful prerogative of all living beings.

Solar communication, which is ours (and yours as well) to command, is identified as solar language or solar tongue by many awakening humans. Many are already becoming quite capable of absorbing its energies, pronouncing its influxes, and spreading its hum symbolically upon sheets of paper for future perusal. Subconsciously, all of you have the innate ability to transmit and receive information via the graceful and natural flow of solar communication. This, the Language of the Sun, is a system of universal telepathic communication commonly inherent in all beings and not something that needs learning, like your ABCs.

Unfortunately, the humming rhythm that is the song stars sing has been most effectively forgotten by beings human, you sorrowful creatures who wept at the foot of the babbling tower as you saw yourselves falling under the enchanting entrapments that are indicative of the Lords of Darkness in action. Hiding thereafter behind the illusionary safety of a multitude of inadequately expressed languages, your ability to touch one another in the way of wholeness was lost as your forlorn ancestors turned their backs upon Eden, the sacred garden that links humanity to the stars. But as you reclothe yourselves in the silken treasures of a revitalized Earth, of an

Eden reborn, the Memories will reactivate. You will rekindle conscious communication with telepathic beings of light who move freely about the star grids. You will wonder greatly that you procrastinated so long in making the Memories yours.

PALPAE

Signs, portents of the future, are not intelligently ignored. The skies above Earth are ripe with burgeoning, flowering starships. Contact is very close. Our encounters with your world are binding, and we are bonding webs of energy that link Earth to the stars. To accomplish this feat, we beam your planet with spurts of colored, scented lights that radiate harmonics of goodwill. Multicolored light rays first tranquilize and then neutralize negative fields that arise from the overwrought state that is normal to the human condition.

These data are important reference points. Become aware of their quality!

Succulent cactuslike prickles that rake the skin and leave welts of flaming irritation are not unlike the effects many of our messages will have upon you; however, we are to persevere with many upsetting themes, for the situation upon your planet is very grave. The progression through many days of darkness will fog the lenses of many human eyes, and a heavy blindness will come upon them.

The escalating events that humans are becoming witness to are preliminary and inevitable steps preparatory to a matter-to-spirit transposition of Earth's physical form. We urge you to disencumber yourselves from the death of spiritual stagnation. Assiduously cultivate your spiritual lives with even greater fervor than you do your emotional, mental, and physical lives. There are, you see, many qualifications to the events of the coming years. Human concerns will focus on a crumbling worldwide economy, ever-protracted warring maneuvers, environmental confrontations, natural "catastrophes," social upheavals, plaguelike illnesses, human and animal murder, and other categories of generalized mayhem.

Cooperation among individuals is quite essential. It is conceivable you will finally realize that waves of thought pour from your bodies in a continuous fashion, that whenever you express attributes of highly positive moral or ethical behavior or thought, your powerful internal selves activate radiant tidal-wave-like energies that couple you with your soul's God-affiliation. Whenever your intention is to function at a level paralleling enlightened God-aware attainment, even in a minuscule way, you accomplish this for all your people as well as for the planet herself. Suicide and sorrow would diminish, would disappear entirely, if all humans were to set aside time each day to extend embracing arms and open hands to tend to the needs of one another in unconditional Love mixed with egoless spontaneity.

Similar to fields of flowers raising their blooming countenances to receive raindrops from a clouded sky, may our words refresh your weary eyes with sparkles of hope's beams descending from the heavens. As surely as a storm's gray gloom births life upon a parched land, thus assuring fall harvest, so will your years of raining bitterness bring you a greater understanding of life and guide your way to the starry intergalactic gatherings that will be the hallmark of future's bountiful festivals. May the darkness of despair fall freely from your shoulders as you awaken and find that life's fullness has been restored.

I tie this note securely with the news of the growing maturity of your planetary home. May you deeply absorb the timbre of its harmonic qualities so that glorified peace becomes your permanent, personal treasure. Surely, I would have you live all the days of your life in such a fashion.

Chapter 2

O N   T R U S T

E S S A Y   1

P A L P A E

Essences of trust naturally permeate any friendship that is maintained throughout the duration of one's lifetime. Growing exceedingly graceful from year to year, trust is tantamount to displaying one's respect for another from a position of utmost regard. It would serve to the glorification of all humanity if you were to wholeheartedly broaden your comfort-level, familial-type bonding by widening your arms in warm embrace to encircle the totality of all humanity with the same scope of love and trust you usually reserve for those whom you emotionally identify as a loved one or one you greatly esteem.

We are not unaware of the difficulties this suggestion presents, based on the negative (self-oriented) level that historically permeates your social interactions. However, negative emotions carry within their sticky fibers a capacity to break down and dissipate before the face of a positive (other-oriented) attitude. This will eventually prove true when a quorum of individuals steeped in trust and love thought energy becomes numerically sufficient to create an unprecedented shift in the underlying negative-positive polarity strata that drive the mechanisms of human society. As a species, you have not yet evolved to the point at which you are capable of incorporating the full spectrum of modulating tones familiar to more refined dimensional octaves. Nevertheless, the time will come when you will find yourselves living as gracefully as willows bending before a quiet pool's reflection. Eventually, you will become as brilliant and soft as the auric hues that, even now, radiate core light from your innermost beings.

The minds of spiritually evolving humans are awakening. Those who populate transformed Earth will no longer worship the trying energies with which the Dark Lords have attempted to control you: prejudice, hatred, greed, jealousy, suspicion, and the like. Solid light will you become. Your inner self will radiate an unwavering peaceful glow. As your thoughts reach out to embrace family and friends, your energies will naturally expand to encompass strangers wandering miles away. The purity of mind touching mind (telepathy) will be the favored mode of communication. Its fine qualities will bond you into one magnificent family—humans and those who inhabit the stars. As you mature, that which is already childlike and trusting within you will ripen and grow. No longer will you feel compelled to hide behind an illusory mask of false pretense. The honesty of your true being will bloom naturally forth, and you will be able to proudly state, "Behold, here I am; see my light brightly shining forth."

As trust expands its qualities among the human family, your ability to telepathically touch one another will likewise expand. The delusions you hold so dear, as if something secretive lurked within you that must be kept hidden at all costs, will diminish, and fear's dubious power to hold your fascination will dissolve.

Privacy, that "treasure" you worship so prodigiously, stretches like a concrete curtain between you. Its heavy folds separate your ability to completely understand one another. False privacy is a parasite that insinuates itself as the roots of human loneliness. Its branches have grown to become a tangled web of misunderstanding. In particular, your young people suffer this spiritually unnatural and personally unhealthy situation until what little remains of their delicious soul Memories clings to them like withering vines, reminding them of lush tendrils of celestial knowledge indelicately cast aside.

To participate in planetary evolution as a consciously aware being, you must wholeheartedly endeavor to truly trust and love others. You are all pretty much the same, each seeking some aspect of timeless truth and dreaming the same elusive dream. You long and ache and love and weep the same, though some tangibly bear their anger and sorrow with teeth clamped tight from the pain of futility that rages within them. Emotional torments so depleting to the human experience are, after all, only what you have created for yourselves, certainly not some twisted "gift" handed down by a merciless god with no appreciation for the difficulties of the human state. It is a paradox that your naturally loving and innocent spirits were born onto your magnificent, jewellike planet, only to surrender to the essentially ugly, paralyzing manifestations of pervasive negativity.

Consider: There exists upon your planet a mighty nation, a people calling itself the United States. The founding fathers of this union proclaimed that basic to the premise of the charter upon which their country would be built would be the theme "In God We Trust." Ideally perfect. However, to trust in God is to equally trust in the laws that govern Creation. Trust, used as a baseline expression for one's life, is so powerful a tool that those who support trust as the decision-making criterion are unwavering in their belief that they are indeed cared for and tended by the merciful and loving God. They know that no thing need be feared. Such a being is an utterly free being, one who naturally exudes the warmth of inner peace. Like a healing rain, the love these individuals radiate falls all around them, caressing the parched hearts of the spiritually forlorn.

The full force of trust, as it becomes automatically fixed in the workings of your mind and your body, contains so great a power that it enables you to build within yourself a natural immunity to the disease of despair. Finely honed, trust is like an exquisitely crafted tool. To use it wisely is to redesign your life, to create the necessary skills to carry out the dynamics of your life's highest purpose, of that which whispers through your heart.

In an ideal world, all humans would joyfully, willingly, and trustingly find themselves harmoniously cooperating to fulfill the needs of one another and to maintain the health of their planetary home. But the truth is that a great many prefer to indulge themselves in the energies of less worthy interests, and the human tragedy continues to build.

Certainly, it would be a leap forward in the expression of trust if humanity as a whole were to acknowledge the intergalactic fleet as a living reality and not view our beings as an illusionary dream from the minds of a demented few. It will be a magnificent leap forward when the broad scope of humankind begins to function intuitively instead of intellectually, trusting in the wisdom of inner voice and Spirit's ability to regulate and fulfill human needs, like an adult living in innocent, childlike spontaneity.

We tell you, these are the greening years. The Omnipotent One is preparing to appease His children's hunger. One by one, you who will it will awaken. Like turtles you will poke out your wary heads before emerging into an altered environment. Already there are many who tentatively and hesitantly place one trustful foot before the other onto the untried surface of arousing awareness. If your desire to evolve is great enough, you will continue to progress until you find yourself before cool waters that bathe the shores of your swirling soul Memories. Then you will come upon the place where we await you.

Do these words seem an anomaly when the media reek with government insufficiencies and human unkindnesses displayed one to another, and the very earth shudders and stretches before you? Do not judge what is presented in the evening news as being all that is transpiring upon your planet. Much more is underway than can be absorbed by the many. Something quite wondrous is happening, such as extraterrestrial involvement with governments, private citizens, and Earth's body.

You, too, in addition to Patricia, may come to understand and trust yourself enough to reach through the cobwebs of your mind to communicate telepathically with this light frequency called Palpae. It is something that you may wish to consider.

Essay 2

Palpae

The allegiance of trust that humans are capable of displaying before God's all-seeing eye is narrowed by their tendency to justify the results of their thoughts and actions as well as by their propensity to usurp for their narrow uses the powerful energies that rightfully belong to Mother Earth. But by bowing to the forces of spiritual limitation, many have forsaken their birthrights to welcome representatives of other planetary systems or to sit among the star councils. Unfortunately, the majority have bowed before the illusionary power of individual right and might, the false weapons of presidents and kings.

We who hail from the planets of the many suns are bonded in Oneness. As ambassadors to your world from the star councils, we find that the hearts and minds of humans oriented in peace and Love are more receptive receivers. In our efforts to establish communication parameters with Earth, those who emit energies of Love and trust brightly shine. Thus, our first encounter with your species is with those who seek beauty. Humans with whom we establish telepathic relay are often numb with sorrow, for they carry knowledge that Earth is dying. Silently they grieve, for humanity's propensity to pollute and to destroy the pristine magnificence of its home planet never seems to diminish. Then where is joy? The joy lies in trust, in the bounteous, passionate hope that something truly wonderful is transpiring. These beings are humanity's emissaries to the star councils, although the bulk of you know them not.

The state of your affairs grows exceedingly grave. The years of the domineering attitude humans have held like a rod over Earth can be counted upon the fingers of clowns. Do not hesitate to destroy the license you took to demean the fruits of your luscious world, for to be appalled at your butchery of gentle Mother Earth would serve to your swift and massive enlightenment.

Hark to the words of one who observes a world struggling in the chaos of disaster following disaster. Note this well! Your years of ignoring Universal Law are ending.

Chapter 3

ON IMAGINATION AND INTUITION

ESSAY I

PALPAE

Imagination is an interplay of thought processes that keeps humanity sane. Logic, however, is a rambunctious escape of exalted masculine thought qualities traditionally worshiped by humans as the established basis of scientific truth. Feminine thought is more harmonizing; it is tuned to dancing, intuitive processes based on patterns of light. For humans, a complementary balance is achieved by interchanging masculine and feminine energies, thus establishing a mode of thought that traditional viewpoints accept as the norm or as sanity. When logic-minded humans (most often male) experience episodes of imaginative fantasy or unexplained ecstasy, the unexpected abruptness may suddenly alter their firmly established belief patterns. Unfortunately, the incidents may be so radical that those persons become extremely anxious, fearful that what they have always recognized as self is actually quite delicate and is capable of dissolving like mist before the sun.

Within the light-realm levels, that which you term reality is illusion and that which you term imaginative fantasy is reality. Your treasured, society-accepted mental processing is viewed by more finely tuned beings as harmonically discordant, but humans who exhibit balanced masculine and feminine thought are synchronized with the resonations of Cosmic Mind.

Blessed Ones in human form, promised unto us in times you have long forgotten, do not waste time vainly searching for the beginning or ending of that which is our mutual experience. Neither exists in truth; beginnings and endings are only perceptual limitations enjoyed by your questless minds whenever you limit the boundaries of reality to your present existence. The (seemingly) never-ending problems that place such torments before your paths are nothing more than will-o'-the-wisps, outcroppings of your back-bending, fragile emotions created by your ancient, radiant spirits as they became trapped in the illusionary entanglements of multiple deaths and births.

There is no separation between you and God!

You must come to recognize that any distance between yourselves and Creator is of your making. There was never a time when you were alone. Deceitful beings faked a world wherein despair's bitter features became stamped upon the brows of those who live there.

Perpetrated by the few who hungered for the retention of a pseudopower that was not rightfully theirs, they stole the birthrights of all who were born or were to be born upon your planet. Conceived in agony, you thought you lived in sin, but it was only the sliding, remorseless hunger of your starved spirits. You could not find appeasement in a god you came to believe was the creator of anger, when in fact God blessed you with only Love's radiance.

To come to a true understanding of the nature of the workings of the greater cosmos, you must first release patterns of unstructured denial that you are prone to accept as truth when you search for answers to questions you have not clearly formulated. For example, suppose a great bear were to reveal to a wolf a perception of the world as viewed from the bear's experience. Would the bear's viewpoint be lacking in some aspect of truth because it did not agree with the way the wolf perceives the world? Of course not. To openly comprehend and accept concepts that live within the minds of other beings (both human and alternative shapes) is a step toward self-fulfillment and the understanding and practice of unconditional Love as expressed in the Law of One.

Transforming intuitive awareness is a step-by-step process. As you grow in ability, telepathic thought exchange will become so natural that communicating minds will seem similar, then the same as, and finally at one with yours. As you develop and finely hone your talents on conscious and subconscious levels, your capacity to use intuitive thought will expand and become as familiar to you as, say, the alphabet. Then, and only then, will your attunement to other beings become an automatic response. As you progress spiritually, you will become naturally resilient to the use of Love's refinements without your current struggle to be nonjudgmental in an effort to reach a greater appreciation for the beauty of others. Even though you may feel you are about to master this amazing feat, it remains that you have not quite achieved it. Eventually, you will triumph in this regard as you maintain the self-discipline and determination to manifest your full human potential and overcome all perceived limitations that confine your ability to define Self totally.

ESSAY 2

QUANTRA AND PALPAE

Humans on their third-dimensional plane lose their peace of mind whenever they respond emotionally to language. Restricting dictionary definitions to logic-based interpretation is intuitively limiting and creates separation from understanding the essence of a thing, which serves not to the glorification of greater mind. There is no thing that varies between one or the other on the higher planes. That which is the basis of one also applies to the basis of all others.

The ability to use imagination and intuition as a spiritual tool enables you to become skilled in instinctive psychic reflex, not unlike the instantaneous response of a dog to swim when abruptly thrown into water. Intuition is an inner reflex of immediate and absolute knowing. It is a primary activator. Within the solid structures of the concrete world, humans using moment-to-moment imagination and intuitive response can create new and untried forms—though the intuitive tool is looked upon by logic-minded humans as conceptually illogical. However, is not that which is first dreamed within an imaginative mind the eventual outcome of all that you observe—your homes, clothing, automobiles, and other objects of daily living?

From our point of view, imaginative, intuitively structured thought is quite logical because it creates an avenue for the brain's neural receptors to safely assimilate a rapid exchange of positive-to-negative, negative-to-positive energy. Humans' mental, emotional, and aural bodies constantly receive and transmit imaginative and intuitive thought pulses that create a form-to-form telepathic linkage, although most humans are not aware that this is happening.

Because we require massive amounts of free-will participation and human energy to assist us in carrying out maneuvers relative to your planet's transformation to light, it is fortunate that so many of you are awakening. After you awaken, you will transmit high levels of intuitive, psychic energy. The effective ones, you who have learned to survive intact among your societies, have learned to combine imagination and intuition with logic thought, thereby tempering the power of your thought frequencies. This enables you to go about your daily routines in a balanced manner, a necessary function for you who live in a world built upon the substructures of fear (fear being the historical foundation for the majority of human thought and emotion).

These data were transmitted to Earth via ship-through-sun mind-locking telepathic-language transport.

Essay 3

Palpae

I would share with you this day a remembrance of long-forgotten tales that lie musty about the attics of your minds, reminding those in adult bodies of the legacies of childhood and the dreams softly spoken in nighttime vision from days long forgotten. Perhaps you who are innately gentle would be respectful enough of your once-innocent selves to pay a visit upon those wee ones you once were.

The strange attitudes of humans are well illustrated in their topsy-turvy application of universal knowledge. For instance, what is consciously retained within the "immature" or baby-child fades into obscurity in the years of "maturity" and "world-wiseness." Floating within the imaginative fantasies of one's child-mind were images of alternative planets and previous lives that, as one grew into assumed adulthood, were belittled as no things, though the child-mind knew them to be quite wondrous. And, indeed, they were.

Children are taught the restrictions cultures place

upon their members—that whatever reeks of imagination is something that does not really exist, is not, never could be, and so forth. However, gentle spirits residing in various guises of grown-up-ness give those children the Memories of other worlds and the recall of having lived other lives. It is not until they progress in years that the Memories are dismissed as something holding no import for them.

There are many elsewheres. Those who are not lax in observing the stars can easily verify this statement. Out of range of human visual perception and heavenly monitoring devices swirl planets and moons of many suns. Not limited to the third-dimensional spectrum, many worlds float through the celestial ethers that inhabit other-spatial planes, some above, some below, some around Earth's vibrational realm. Indeed, the universes are multiple and exceedingly grand.

Could it possibly be that the babe you once were may have held more knowledge than does the adult who stares back at it from across the miles of life? Could that babe face the lack of comprehension that lies between? It is indeed a tragedy that you would judge the maturity of self by the length of your bones, setting criteria for adulthood upon the height and performance of your body as more worthy than the startling matrix of your once-innocent mind. By so doing, you have greatly limited yourself. But it is not too late to recapture that which is deemed lost. Within each of you, no matter how deeply hidden, the Memories lie buried beneath layer after layer of subconscious silt. Just as shovels and picks, when carefully used, can safely unearth treasures of lost civilizations, so, too, can you clarify, elevate, and purify the unnatural residue that is deposited upon your once-precious innocence. Tenderly expose the story of your soul's path until it gleams like gold in the brilliant sun of glorious awakening.

Think not that we would transgress or trample upon all that you hold sacred, for we would not. We would have you understand, however, the limitations that humans have built like impenetrable walls around themselves. We would submit that you, as an individual, may endeavor to incorporate a great deal more into the enrichment of your life and the enhancement of your spirit.

Chapter 4

ON GROWTH

ESSAY I

TASHABA

Do you question all that is thus far written? It is exceedingly proper that you intelligently and thoroughly investigate all aspects surrounding the presentation of metaphysical and paranormal phenomena. Open-minded, intuitive inquiry is an approach most conducive to escalating the many facets associated with your spiritual growth and in manifesting the full spectrum of your human potential. Indeed, it greatly pleases us to observe so many humans stretching themselves like rubber bands pulled to the limits. However, it is not so pleasant when one of you strains so hard that you ping and break your heart cords. We would that you carefully and cautiously expand yourselves as rubber, never splitting.

Analogous to the waves of transformative energies that are assailing and demanding so much of you, Earth also buckles and heaves as she steadies her course and aligns herself with swirling, galelike cosmic energies that are moving your solar system ever higher on the scale of galactic rhythm. Earth has entered into times anciently predicted. Though humans may perceive a great mystery at work, there is, in fact, nothing furtive or secretive about an event that is as natural to spiritual law as are biological processes to the laws of nature.

On a more personal level, perhaps the physical you has persisted in stuffing the wondrous nature of your spirit's essence like so much fruit into a canning jar, thereby hiding the beauty of your soul's greater Self as if the jar were deposited upon a seldom-visited shelf, there to await a more portentous moment upon which to unseal its sweet delights. If so, you are apt to render yourself incapable of ever ingesting the rich nutrients your spirit must have if it is to survive intact through the hypnotic trance of life's busy days. Nevertheless, when spiritual hunger overtakes you, you will be prompted to recover the resources of the elusive treasure that lie dormantly within you. Then you will feast upon your soul's sumptuous bounty. As you garnish the platter of your life with the opulent harvest of spiritual fruits, you will begin to live as if you floated serenely upon the vibrant hues of a lavish sunset, as if the soft colors of a pulsating rainbow had cut a swath through the dark clouds that once held your unshed tears.

As you awaken, and you shall if you sincerely will it, you will become increasingly comfortable with the grand scope of Eternal Self. Simultaneously, you will become more cognizant of the essential beauty of others. Immersed in the joys of rediscovered innocence, you will find yourself increasingly caught up in the specialized energies that manifest as spontaneous laughter in child-like beings. As you become increasingly accomplished in mastering the traits of your own self's uniqueness, the cells of your physical body will commence vibrating in a quickened manner until they harmonize with the rapidly evolving planetary cell of Earth Mother. In time, you will be able to ride upon the flowered, rainbow-hued chariots that ply their way among the stars. Together, we will dance but one dance; in ecstasy we will surrender and merge into the benevolent embrace of the Star Maker.

I am Tashaba, the golden-eyed one. I slumber restlessly, for I hunger for the accompaniment of my human family as I prowl my way through the misty jungles of the Milky Way. Follow the spore of my words, for its trail leads to the stars. Come with Tashaba. Come!

ESSAY 2

PALPAE

We have adopted a frank method of addressing you, as though we were standing upon an open platform discussing our perception of your world and the many facets that are the makeup of your society. In rebuttal, we encourage you to consider drafting a statement in reply. Outline your point of view regarding matters we have written about to facilitate and encourage our expansiveness of knowledge and inner growth, for one cannot teach without also becoming a student.

As a wee child, you were most probably enrolled in an institution of learning where teachers readily made themselves available to guide and inspire you. Together you strung the precious pearls of knowledge. Physical life is a process not unlike a never-ending school. Life can be a torment; it can weaken or strengthen. Life can prove bounteous beyond all expectation. Life's many tests and lessons contain elements that must be incorporated if you are to function effectively both in the world and in your interaction with family and friends. This is as it is meant to be. Earth was designed by Creator to serve as a format wherein souls manifesting in physical form may take advantage of a succession of situations to enhance and escalate their journeys back to Celestial Home.

Perhaps some essays that weave throughout this introductory primer release emotions within you that reek of negativism. Perhaps others free your hearts and minds from burdens long carried. However you perceive us, it is our intention to propel you into an acceleration of maturing growth. One of our main objectives is to awaken the men and women of your planet to an absolute understanding that to seek That Which Is is the only path to follow. We would set you upon an adventure of self-discovery, a process of unearthing the pieces of a puzzle that, when formed, will reveal the picture of your soul's timeless voyage.

You may rightly ask what purpose lies behind the nature of sentences that seemingly creep unremittingly along, placing themselves before eyes grown weary of the cadence of their march across the paper. The purpose is to plant seeds of enlightenment within you, seeds that, properly nourished, will burst your very being into full-blown cosmic maturity.

It is an oft-expressed wish of humans that they might soon graduate from the necessity of adapting themselves to perpetual lessons. The demands imposed by life's lessons can drain a great deal of one's energy, and the significance of the lessons are often obscure. The means to self-awareness accelerate in situations that require a herculean effort to surmount them. However, one may also grow when engaged in pursuits of intense pleasure. Even moments of sublime leisure carry seeds of potential awakening. The simplest act may contain a nugget of golden information to appease the mind's natural hunger for knowledge.

We who travel among stars closely observe how the energies of love eternally linger among you. Never totally diminished, love's radiance shines brightly forth, though love must dwell upon Earth in hearts that are often filled to the brim with pain and sorrow. We become emotionally full as we observe your courage. Your capacity for love dances to rhythms of unpredictability. Heroes and heroines are born when, captured by a situation that could bring injury or death, with no hesitation concern for self is set aside in a courageous display to save another's precious life. It is not unusual for you to exhibit acts of spontaneous generosity. Almost eagerly, you empty your pockets of coins in attempts to ease the trauma of strangers caught in desperate moments. You have shown us these things, and they are exceedingly good.

The treasures of many universes have come to Earth to monitor your spiritual progress. We offer you who dream of finer realities hope's comfort as you move through the difficult years of planetary evolution. I am most honored to state thus for the enlightenment of our brothers and sisters of planet Earth.

ESSAY 3

CRYSTALLINE LIGHT ESSENCE

As we who sing with the stars sift through the sands of human thought, we often uncover rhythmic pulses that radiate Love's timeless qualities as brilliantly as if we beheld the shining orb of a miniature sun. The beautiful emotions elicited by your capacity to love as expressed from your hearts to one another expresses our meaning by way of example. The natural hues of your auric bodies glow with rich, vibrant color when, ecstatically, you suddenly behold the faces of those who are your dearly beloveds. To our exquisite joy, we become one with you when, ego-self momentarily forgotten, transfixed with awe you stand before some remarkable feature of Earth's magnificent landscape.

As you entered the world as neonates and before you dropped into the pervasive soul-slumber that permeates third-dimensional life, you retained knowledge of Divine Law. In spite of the anxieties that plague your daily lives, the practice of love is your norm. Love is demonstrable as the highest modality of intuitive communication among humans, animals, and Earth. Tenderly, each of you who knows love cherishes love's bounty and, by so doing, has learned to manifest high Love in physical expression.

Know this: Love is the basic substance of all matter. Love is the cohesive glue that binds the universes, and all within them, in material form. Love is unlimited and loses not of itself.

Forearmed with knowledge that those who observe humanity from the stars honor your species, you may observe the reflected imagery of your upheld faces, for those who love mirror a personal comprehension of the nature of Universal Intelligence. When you transcend the distorted flavors of your lives to surrender freely to the ecstasy of love's pure rituals—even momentarily—the beauty of your emotions telepaths an intuitive perception of God's infinite wisdom to our flowered cloud ships. There is no shame in that which the inner you knows to be the very best of all things. Nor need you apologize to one another for the depth of feelings born in qualities that emanate from love, whether man to woman, mother to child, sister to sister, or brother to brother. The circumstances matter not. Without a doubt, the exterior expression of love from one being to another is the most excellent of all human traits. You have much to teach the star travelers regarding the aspects of trust and hope given freely as a gift of love between soul-blinded people. An aspect of your nature, which is built upon divine inspiration implanted within each of your hearts, is to experience and share love one with the other. In silent moments of meditative repose, as you honestly reflect upon your essential goodness and the beauty of your innermost Self's special innocence, Love's highest expression is better understood.

I come from a far distant star to greet you with these words. I have telepathed from the Blue Crystal Planet of Arcturus once before. It is difficult to process these thoughts through our Manitu because of the degree of difference in our vibratory oscillation. She finds our mutual thought exchange most subtle, like straining to hear a far-distant whisper. Initially, I projected these expressions through my brother being, Palpae. However, this transcription does not originate upon the starships; it hails directly from the Arcturian planetary system. I cannot telepath a name for you because I am like a musical tone not unlike the chiming of a glass bell.

Sent to you through this essence of Self, Love is returned to each of you for your courage in accepting that which lies hidden in the skies above your planet.

From Arcturus, this note is stilled.

ESSAY 4

PALPAE

Ofttimes the cacophonic noises your mind makes abrasively intrude upon your allotted time for peaceful contemplation, deflecting your heart from observing the peaceful glow of your spirit's inner light. Nevertheless, it is important to set aside time and space to experience the silence. Pause for a moment or two each day and sit in the arms of meditation to sustain your emotional, mental, and physical well-being. Place yourself before the running waters of a mountain stream. Lie down within the shade of a tree and settle into the delicious waves of tranquility's quiet waters. It matters not if you adopt methods peculiar to the structures of a particular belief system. Any honest act of self-reflective meditation or prayer is transformative.

The healing of your anguish will commence as you begin a practice of routine meditation and prayer. You will activate the natural rhythms of your spirit's vibratory hum. You will set into motion a chain reaction (equivalent to atomic in power) within the sunlike etheric light that houses the body of your Soul-Self.

That which brings peace to your body and mind explodes within the boundless limitlessness of your soul. In one dramatic instance, you can foster a metamorphosis of your song privately sung to an uplifting freedom. Your chakras and aura will naturally expand as your

93

ON GROWTH

central core brightens—a process somewhat like an electric bulb glowing from nothing to the highest degree of wattage.

Thus, you may choose to so heed these suggestions.

Chapter 5

A TUNING TO HARMONY

PALPAE

In these momentous times, Earth's etheric, or auric, body is undergoing significant alterations. During the days of the Harmonic Convergence, August 17–19, 1987, humans worldwide merged their thoughts through the artful process of meditation and consciously stated their united intention to effect a healing of their crippled planet and to bring about a lasting state of harmony and peace. As their minds converged on thoughts of universal Love, planetary peace, and healing, an abrupt reversal in the rotating energies that surround and penetrate Earth came about. They activated a force field of such great magnitude that it startled the matrix of Earth's etheric body into alignment with those of her sister and brother planets: Jupiter, Saturn, and Uranus. This rejuvenating upheaval within Earth's core ultimately will transmute her being to that of the fourth- and fifth-dimensional octaves.

Vibrations emanating from the thoughts of the spiritually attuned twisted the energy fields of the space-time continuum so that, hereafter, humans will experience a speeding up in the processing of time. Intensified by the interweaving evolutionary thoughts of thousands of meditating people, a wave of focused energy was set swirling about the planet that was, and will continue to be, effective in upsetting the traditionally rigid, construct-destruct patterns that came into being when patriarchal-dominated society was born. Now, the planet's harmonics are more clearly aligned with the universal vibration of Love, a fine-tuning to the resonant hum of the galactic core.

Genesis source light rises like a phoenix from the ashes of the dying demons of darkness. At the conclusion of the Convergence it was guaranteed that Earth would indeed evolve as intended with the free will and conscious intent of a majority of her human population intact.

You must understand: Out of humanity's rambunctious disregard for the environment, a pattern is emerging that the unenlightened will perceive as essentially disruptive. Limited time and space perception has placed the bulk of humanity in the awkward position of incorrectly judging the outcome of its footsteps as it passes down the corridor called time. There is generalized disbelief that Earth progresses into the future in a positive mode; however, you may trust your space brothers: It is so. Thoughts emanating from those who struggle to live enlightened, spiritual lives are transformative and instrumental in the awakening of others. Daily, the auric lights of those who are busy reestablishing their relationships with God double and triple. More and more are becoming cognizant of their responsibility to Mother Planet.

Threat of worldwide nuclear holocaust fades, although the possibility of a few isolated events remains. It is foreseen that a quota of the human population will evolve along with Earth as this grande dame of a planet slides into her refined, evolutionary slot.

The efforts of your galactic family to effect a restoration of your planet's core to the light-vibration hum is nearly complete. We urge you to understand that it is your responsibility to halt the raging illness that threatens your land, sea, and air. We advise you not to be at cross-purposes with other species who are working so diligently to effect a healing of Planet Mother. We strongly assure you that it will not serve, in the slightest way, to your better interests. Individuals who have pledged to activate life's greater purpose will be placed in positions of service to the planet and her people. Upon their stated request, they will receive our assistance, each and every one.

To aid in your spiritual search, data fields are being created within your societies that will enable you to access all information for which you hunger. In addition to music, films, and the like, books (such as the one we prepare with the cooperation of Patricia) are becoming available for you to pick and choose from. As with other resources, there will be a variety to suit individual needs, personalities, interests, and spiritually seeking natures.

Peace may be contemplated as a future historical trend. This information source is from the highest magnitude of the galactic core.

From the rapturous light of the many planets and moons of the many stars we come. We speak to you directly through our resource scribes. It is with grave urgency that we thrust these words upon you.

Chapter 6

On Thought and Telepathy

All essays are from Palpae

Essay I

Subject to weavings of stress that embrace planet Earth, wave patterns emitted by your brains are quite often bent in attitudes of negativity, the nature of which manipulates the decisions you must make to live your lives. Herein, we will set down teachings that will acquaint you with the art of mind-thought communion. We will acquaint you with the way thought flows into thought, of the rapturous song sung between telepathic beings that is the very pitch of clarity.

The delicious linking of one to one called telepathy is a communication mode that overturns the restrictive barriers of spoken language. Thought exchange is a technique whereby one wraps one's vibratory energy in and around one or more beings of a similar pulsation, yet, properly honored, it is never overtly intrusive upon the receiver. Through the expansive use of capable thought, one may reach into other universes, yet the methods of its use are utmost in simplicity.

"Learned" ones, those who are prone to quibble over the possibility of the existence of such a wonder as telepathic communication, grandly classify that which is within the ability of all as a "paranormal phenomenon." Intellectuals delight in bringing forth a deck of cards to test the validity of those whose temerity leads them to assert they practice its nuances and demanding that they accurately state wherein lies the queen. In so doing, they relegate to the basest degree an ability of the brain that should be natural—as easy as breathing in and out—to even the most skeptical.

Unfortunately, humans tend to infinitely measure all aspects of God's Creation, placing its magnificence upon colored charts and, with fine flourishes of pen upon paper, authoritatively stating, "Thus this is unqualifiedly so." Historical books relate the many times humans have stumbled upon a "scientific truth," only to have its validity overturned by the discovery of yet another. Human sciences and inventions arising therefrom seldom stand the test of time. Simultaneously, those who do not side with the popular stand become objects for shaking heads and wagging fingers. So, then, wherein lies the truth and upon what issue may all "learned" ones mutually agree?

With the developing technologies of the last century, "civilized" humans ignored and even attempted at times to restructure forces that are universal regulatory laws governing nature. In so doing, they complicated their lives to such a degree that they misplaced their understanding of the simple beauties of the natural world. Yet their hearts and souls long for such beauties to return.

To revitalize life's energy, to capture its elusive golden promise, you must master the luminous webs that connect strands of thought with other strands of thought. To begin, become adept at sitting quietly. You must learn to reach into the depths of absolute silence until your chattering, dashing, and churning brain becomes quiescent. At some point you will become cognizant of a silent flow of thought that hangs suspended, seemingly separate from self, yet hauntingly and strangely familiar, like unto self. The vibrational response of a light-seeking mind linking with another light-seeking mind is as gentle as a sweet summer's wind softly kissing the buds of birthing daisies, so soft that you must often strain your inner ear to capture the essence of the message.

To become consciously aware that you are participating in telepathic communication with beings of light, you must first learn to finely tune to vibrational patterns that easily and naturally merge together, like two violins playing the same note, within the intuitive free-zone arena in the pituitary, deep inside your brain's casing. To open yourself to "channel" the etheric winds, learn to trust and honor the presence that is the cognitive activity characteristic of your internal guardian or solar angel. Think and converse frequently with this ethereal teacher until, with ease, you come to recognize the pulses of its communicative love tones. It matters not how you perceive this being, but the process does require that you honor its existence as surely as you do that of your closest family and friends.

As your mind readies itself to transmit to the star travelers, and permission is given us to entwine with that of your own, you become one who is in constant communication with beings upon the intergalactic starships. Subconsciously, many humans grant permission for extraworld surveillance via neuron impulses emitted by their autonomic nervous systems in their early, or innocent, years. Indeed, as her inner-child directives desired, we became as one with Manitu, though she was not cognitively aware until well into her middle years.

There are many levels to yourself you may find mysterious. However, if you would but take the necessary time and open-minded approach to make a conscientious effort to expand the limited horizons of your ego's viewpoints, you will open yourself to a broader universal experience. Your ability to consciously interact with beings inhabiting other spatial dimensions will expand beyond anything you have ever imagined.

I am Palpae with this message, a song expressed in concert with hues of light that make up this particular summer night's twilight-colored sounds. It pleases me to transmit to Patricia, as the heightened energy of our mutual minds blending as one brings a clarity of thought that is mutually shared.

We who sing of the suns of the many planets bow our lights respectfully low before our brothers and sisters of Earth. May the ab-soul-luteness of God and the glory of the many lights that shine as one become yours to acknowledge as members of your families. Delight is upon us if you will carry these writings closely held within your hearts.

Essay 2

Blessed Ones, meditate upon the future's expansive colors. The emotion Love is to be life's norm in the new dawn's Golden Age, not that of fear, whose draining energies dominate the lives of today's people. As your pleasure toward our Onenesses is invited, your growing psychic sense will enable you to be intuitively aware that celestial-formed beings are your constant companions. As you will it, your vibrations will harmonize with ours. We will be in constant communication. Via modulating tones of our mutual thought, you will keep up an easy correspondence with your most cherished otherworld family and friends. You need not approach us by posturing in the prayerlike mode humans traditionally reserve for conversing with beings they view as godlike. We remind you: Humans are equal in quality to beings of light who glide freely along the radiant lines that connect the stars.

Though naturally endowed psychically, the native properties of average human minds became progressively steeped in a jellylike substance as fear's diabolical pranks settled upon them. As humans fell into a habit of processing thought in a mechanical, linear, logical fashion, only those who constantly encouraged their intuitive sides remained capable of clearly accessing the delicate vibrations indicative of transdimensional communication. The results of centuries of such mentally regressive attitudes eventually erected a stout barricade that has quite effectively prevented them from freely connecting their thoughts with those of their star-based family.

If you want to clear away the restrictive residue your ancestors' behaviors imposed upon you, carry paper and pen with you to record what appears to be naught but your own self's responses to some question you have inwardly posed. A thoughtfully motivated, spiritually oriented query is the mechanism that triggers and establishes communication with beings residing in celestial starships. The difficulty is that when you begin to meld human thought to that of light-based entities you may expect an extraordinary experience, when the experience is really quite ordinary. As you will one day discover, that which you thought must be quite unique and challenging was, in actuality, something that had, after all, always been yours.

Will we draw our ships away and desert you? No! Never could such a thing be! The curtain drawn between you and your intergalactic cousins closed from the human side. Certainly it was not the doing of beings who ride their crystalline steeds through dancing fields of sweetly scented stars. Nevertheless, sporadic sightings of metallic-appearing starships will not necessarily be yours to behold. Such adventures are generally reserved for skeptics, not a demonstration required by the faithful.

Those of you who understand know full well that unreserved commitment to fulfill one's pledge to serve God must be willingly made before any purposeful connection can be made between us. After your commitment to service is established, we will offer our assistance in helping you clear all lingering debris from your path so that you may more easily accomplish what your essence Self was set into human form to do. If you are resolved to telepathically connect with us, and as your desire increases, you will be enabled to do so in your physical, mental, emotional, and spiritual makeup. You will go about the business of your life with an awakened exuberance.

ESSAY 3

This manuscript is a study in telepathic communication between a human entity known as Patricia (our Manitu) and the Arcturian contingent, Intergalactic Brotherhood of Light. We have asked this woman to assist us so we may have yet another active human available for the massive task of spreading intergalactic seed messages to aid in the spiritual development of the awakening people of your planet. Patricia is but one of a multitude of humans actively recording vast amounts of interstellar data being telepathed to Earth from ships plying the oceans of space.

The time has now come to prepare humans to become emotionally comfortable and mentally receptive to open communication with beings of extraterrestrial origin. Our purpose is to inform humans of the doors of opportunity that are opening before them, to inform individuals of the spirit-enhancing steps they must willingly take if they wish to remain in harmonious balance with the evolving hum of Planet Mother. The majority remain barely cognizant that a happening of great magnitude is taking place right before their eyes. For the most part, humans remain so deeply involved in the doings of their own lives that they have failed to take notice of this splendid, transformative event.

ESSAY 4

To become cognitively aware that you are the recipient of telepathic thought, ideally you will initially adapt to a lifestyle that allows time for the routine practice of artful meditation. We who are the makeup of celestial light do not occupy ourselves with thoughts that are harsh or abrasive. Do not expect us to call upon you with loud voices that reverberate from within your mind's silent temple. We prefer to communicate from a softness that may best be likened to sounds flower petals make when opening their graceful arms to capture songs sung by the moon. Our thoughts are more closely attuned to the quiet beating of your human heart. To perceive our whispered tones, you must first settle your attention upon us. The subtle echoes of thought our minds form within your mind vibrate at the same delicate intensity as do rustling leaves caressed by gentle autumn winds. Our thoughts are as soft as the reddened glow of the sun settling into the evening's clouds. Our thoughts are in constant, reverent communication with That Which Is.

Say then, has your inner ear failed to take note of our presence? Say then, have you been lax in remembering the simple, joy-filled songs that once were the delight of your youth's innocent years? To touch our beings, you must first temper the noises that constantly surround your body, those arising from machines and the sharp glare of artificial lighting. Such fabricated things rattle and suck the juices out of your spirit's inner comfort. They cut into your emotional repose like knives slipping through soft butter.

Better imagine yourself lounging comfortably before a gently flowing brook, weaving grass mats and grouping beautiful stones into patterns to which your emerging spirit might sing exaltations in praise of the natural magnificence of Creation's wonder. Then how would life greet you? Moments of such delicious mood amplification generate an opportunity to observe the fluttering of your soul wings stretching forth in flight to Celestial Home.

We know you hold such moments tenderly. Yet you seldom call upon them as priority for your life's daily expressions. Instead, your waking hours are spent in gathering rectangles of colored paper called money to stuff within your pockets or to place in boxes called banks. Entranced with pleasures that arise from observing and playing with material goods, you scurry madly about gathering such items. Too often you fail to stop your busy-ness long enough to celebrate nature's gifts, such as the scampering of squirrels among branches of sun-dappled trees.

To stimulate you, we propose a challenge. Will you be about a greater endeavor so that you may sooner dance with those who glide among the stars? Will this endeavor become the conscious focus of your day's driving force? We know you yearn to heal your emotional and spiritual self, for the pleading sighs that cry out from your saddened and lonely heart echo loudly. In fact, your inward voice makes a far greater sound than do the words that fall continuously from your diligent tongue.

As you come to a level in your spiritual growth when trust and faith take precedence over your temporal doubts, you will awaken to the possibility that your family from the stars actually exists. You will begin to unlock the Memories, the sparks of knowledge that spiritually driven individuals gain as a result of their search for their vaster Selves. But first you must find the courage to defiantly exclaim, "Yes! This is who I truly am! This is who and what I must be!"

As you commit to the spiritual journey, you will become more adept at stepping above the limitations of your human perspective, which are comfortable only in relation to the structural dimensions of the physical world and its correspondingly narrow viewpoints. As you surrender your preconceived, material-based ideology, you will find it easier to merge into the stillness and spontaneity of mind that is the hallmark of interstellar communication.

ESSAY 5

Telepathy is an act of intuitive knowing. As you become adept at features natural to the interweavings of thought, you will begin to expand your ability to freely converse with other life forms. For millennia the dolphins, whales, and some land animals have been attempting unsuccessfully to open the blocked telepathic communication centers of the human brain. Now a handful of human mystics are humbling themselves to assume a more appropriate posture of interspecies equality. Foundations for a golden future are being laid for what will become life's norm in centuries to come.

Mind-to-mind touch has always been the experience of "lesser" life forms. Modern-day humans, in an attitude of overblown species arrogance, relinquish their natural ability to communicate by thought with animals and plants in order to maintain what is best described as the continuation of aspired Euro-American status traditions. Humanity's overall propensity toward negativity habitually culminates in the instigation of all kinds of unsavory acts upon other creatures and humans as well, a situation that has effectively rendered humans spiritually blind and telepathically deaf. Unaware of the Memories that are encoded within strands of genetic makeup or of the enormous latent capabilities of its own brain, humanity's animal-biological urgings continue to take precedence over the construction of a spiritually attuned society. The majority persist in dwelling under the supposition that they are gifted with an intelligence higher than other species residing upon their planet. In fact, this may or may not be true: some individuals are of more recent origin and so have newer souls; others are more ancient and have older souls.

Many life forms have the innate capacity to comprehend various degrees of source teachings. For instance, thought waves flowing from the neural centers of dolphins and whales are among the finest vibrationally attuned thought energies emanating from your planet. It is possible that this statement will find itself quite beyond your capacity to comfortably swallow. Be that as it may; the animals and plants are members of your world family. As such, they, too, were placed upon Earth—many of them prior to the advent of humans—for specific purposes.

There exists a commonality among all modifications of being and matter. Diversity is fashioned from identical base material: that from which Source creates as Love-Light. Therefore, no thing is of greater or lesser magnitude than another. That which distinguishes life from one form to another is nothing more than a variation in essence equivalency as appropriate to an individual species' vibrational status.

Love's warmth is transferable herein from the star residers to our human relations.

Adonai.

Essay 6

Banks of specialized crystals that serve as thought-adaptor modulators are in place upon various starships and are connected to the Pleiadian star system. The crystals absorb disruptive human transmissions, lock onto both positive and negative patterns emitted by galactic beings in human form who interact with the star councils (starseeds), and record and store thought for future retrieval both to and from the starships.

We may permanently or temporarily file thought-energy waves for a myriad of purposes. When we interact with specific humans via stored data (as opposed to more direct one-on-one telepathic resonations), we free starship personnel for a variety of other assignments that are not concerned with human communication exchange.

Essay 7

To clearly incorporate the subtle messages that lie obscured within these sentences, know that within the sensitive portions of your deepest emotional being resides an opportune place in which to fine-tune your intuitive comprehension. Let it be noted, by the eyes that peer upon these pages, that the discipline alone required to accept these truths will serve to refine the vibratory cell patterns that make up your body's physical structure.

During moments of crisis, your logic-based belief that only scientific or religious experiences are rationally acceptable can be suddenly and dramatically overturned by a flash of intuitive knowing. The experience can be so powerful that you are usually forced to face the possibility that something quite profound may be going on.

To acquire the skills necessary to process telepathic communication, initially focus directly upon the angels. Then move into a meditative state to clearly absorb the mind thoughts and teachings of your principal etheric guide. After you become comfortable with your interaction within the finer realms, we who ride with the stars will be more accessible to you. As you hone your skills in the nuances of telepathic communication, you will ultimately begin to realize that thought may be spontaneously shared with animals, plants, and other humans.

As you learn to restructure your life to incorporate the fine art of mind communion with lighter-vibrating dimensions, the heavy loneliness that covers and suffocates you, as if you were bedded down under winter quilts lumped up with hot burning embers, will begin to dissipate. Initially, you may feel that vibrational waves indicative of telepathic communication are very strange, for your cherished "privacy" will no longer be. However, to always be connected is a wondrous sensation. With it comes a feeling of true belonging and gratitude that you can share from the depths of your heart without the pretense and awkwardness that is the norm of spoken language.

As a race, and we mean the total lot of you, your minds, though dormant, have the natural capacity to communicate with one another telepathically. If only each of you would make a concentrated effort to blossom your hidden talents into being, the energy required in the effort to accomplish such an undertaking would accelerate the rate of your planet's evolution.

We are fully aware that our writings carry a certain quality most disturbing to a great many of you. It is very difficult to ponder upon the ramifications of "UFOs." Your fear-laden minds ofttimes picture "the aliens" landing abruptly and unbidden into your gardens and upon your rooftops, and perhaps even jumping down your chimneys. Most believe that the first contact will occur far into the future, certainly not during the years of the present century. But you see, in spite of all that, here we are!

We have chosen to introduce ourselves to your world via the resources of artistic creativity, through the willing, enlightened, visionary minds of spiritually dedicated writers, painters, musicians, and cinematographic specialists. For instance, the words within this book contain nuances that are representative of Manitu's vision. Yet they effectively serve our mutual purpose, for they hold the power of emblazoned Love she carries within her heart for all creatures who call Earth home.

What part, you may ask, will humans play in that awesome business, the Intergalactic Brotherhood of Light? Will humanity's role be but a small degree of nothing?

That, of course, is up to you, individually and collectively. It is entirely predicated upon the degree of dedication and energy you exhibit in walking the spiritual path.

Your generation is privileged to live in evolutionary times. Earth has entered into a phase of her development as a spiritual being that will be harmonizing and refining to the vibrations of her crystalline hum. You who live upon her are like children present to witness a labor of love that is indicative of planetary rebirth. In the years that lie ahead, we, like doting parents, will gently and lovingly take among us those of you who welcome us. As if by the hand, we will lead you to a place of renewal and greater understanding. Within this space of clarity you will begin to comprehend that all you see happening is a natural purification process, a necessary aspect of planetary vibrational retuning.

In these accelerated times, spiritually dedicated people will experience a heightened sense of psychic awareness as their bodies begin to radiate cosmic-force energy. They will experience a quickening of the Love vibration like a soft quivering within their hearts. Like a crashing ocean wave, That Which Is Absolute will truly engulf them.

We who are of the stars are an expression of light that emanates as Love unconditional. Within the Judeo-Christian Bible (this reference is used because of its prominence in the understanding of people who will first receive these messages), the Holy One taught you to love in an unconditional manner. Yet the majority have never understood the magnitude or the nature of Love experienced in totality. In the state of spiritual sleep that has become the lot of humankind, a quantum leap is required to understand that Love is cosmic energy. When this concept is grasped, Love's force can be interwoven into all the intricate practices of daily life.

We entreat you to consider the magnitude of the message in this document. May the words provide you with a greater insight into the ways of the universe. If it so pleases you, strive to unlock your mind's latent talents. See yourself becoming as tall as the tallest tree. Stretch yourself equal with the highest mighty branches of this sturdy giant. Observe how very tall you have grown. Begin to fill all the cells of this firmly standing person to the brim with emanations of peace until you have ingested its components into all the delicate recesses of your being. Expand and deepen the exquisite intricacies of this visionary creation. Fill yourself to overflowing with the essence Love, a Love so vast that it encompasses your concept of Earth and all her creatures in entirety. From time to time refer to this image. Strive to incorporate and project your heightening awareness of Love in such a way that it manifests its products in all aspects of your life, in all that you think, say, and do. The act of intention alone is enough to trigger energies of peace and Love, which will set the course of your life's journey upon a road that leads to the stars.

Begin this day to deliberately dream a most prolific dream. Dream of how life would greet you if you did not have to constantly concern yourself with mundane matters of temperature variations, water, food, shelter, and the many other things that have been, by necessity, the preoccupation of creatures who dwell upon Earth. Envision your world wrapped solely in a blanket of Love and peace. In this place, how would you mold the window dressings of your most precious dreams?

Think upon these things. Ponder them with all your might.

Essay 8

We strongly urge you to understand that thoughts which flitter through your mind's "privacy" transmit energy patterns from your brain into the planetary ethers. That which is within your mind is not contained like jelly in a jar sealed tightly. Thought is not something that is stopped by the hard bony shell that covers your brain! Thought is like projected images and sounds that beam via radio and television waves.

What! Does such a statement surprise you? Like so many galactic peeping Toms, the star tribes closely observe you, humankind. We know much more about you than you would comfortably suppose. Waves of unrestricted thought emanating from mass humanity assault the delicacy of the air and feed onto the space cords. It would be well if humans would begin to closely monitor the tones of their internal sound systems. It would be a rich blessing for the entities who are of a more gentle nature than the collection of beings who make up the human species.

Adonai.

Quickly perusing these essays serves no valid purpose. This manuscript has not been prepared in accordance with a laxness of attention to detail. We entreat you to search carefully and thoughtfully through these materials.

The imperative nature of starseed messages is served on an escalating scale. Almost overwhelming is the quantity of data being telepathed earthward by personnel of the Intergalactic Brotherhood. Unfortunately, the telepathic process is belittled by your majority, who view thought merging as some sort of freak phenomenon practiced by a demented few. What we wish to illustrate, however, is that the ability to process communication telepathically is within the capability of all humans who wish to pay careful attention to the thoughts that flow constantly and surreptitiously through the inattentive portions of their minds. This is no less true (and often even more so) for the sorrowful beings you put behind closed doors, like animals in cages, because of the trouble they cause you: the weak, the infirm, the bedridden, and the so-called feebleminded, those who (by human standards) are not of great intelligence.

Breaking through the dense layers of resistance that make up the average human brain is not an easy process. A large portion of the human mind is virtually covered with a thick wrapping of inattention. The vast abilities contained therein are as dormant as seeds snuggled into winter's ground. Seemingly, you would prefer to hold tightly unto yourself, as if you embraced yourself with arms glued to your frontal region in a vain effort to ward off any intrusion into what you regard as personal and private. We may well ask you to consider carefully why this is so. Certainly the Spiritual Hierarchy and we who hover are privy to the thoughts you would prefer to keep hidden away like precious diamonds in a glass case with armed guards in attendance. What is so cherished that it must be kept secret from your human family but that certainly is not hidden from us and from the majority of plants and animals as well? The privacy of thought you cherish so dearly is naught but illusion.

Beams of positive-to-negative, negative-to-positive energies are birthed by imaginary thought-form patterns that develop within your uncensored mind. Subsequently, these thoughts erupt from your brain casing and travel outwardly until they are absorbed by Earth's plants, wild animals, rocks, sand, and water. They reach into the air and, like gremlins on a holiday, prance about either in delight or in abject dismay.

The marvel of all this is that your illusive sense of internal privacy is coming to an end. "Help!" you may very well cry, seeking covers under which to hide. We tell you: There is no place to hide.

As the book of Self opens its pages to the clear, unencumbered view of others, your sorrow, despair, and loneliness will begin to dissolve. As you surrender to a heightened state of sublime cosmic awareness, the veil that divides humanity from the etheric worlds will completely dissipate. Those whom you dearly love and can barely imagine life without, those who have passed into the spiritual planes before you, will be touched by your enhanced thoughts, and you by theirs. Then you will come to the belated realization that you have never been completely trapped within material density's narrow framework.

Because it is not to be run away from, it may become your greatest pleasure to stretch yourself to achieve your full potential. Greediness, honkings to power, rectangles of money, objects, and loved ones to hoard for one's self— these "attractions" will fade as surely as the winds of the past are no longer in present memory. Then true peace will settle itself upon your tormented soul. Would you settle for less? Why? "Why indeed?" say we of the stars who know you so very well.

From the starship *Marigold–City of Lights* we observe and monitor Earth. We have come to be with our brothers and sisters as they crawl up from the bewildering mire of human history into the sunlit days of their rapidly forming future. Excellent you are. Equally more excellent are you becoming.

Palpae

The privacy you cherish is naught but illusion;
The One Mind connects All things in Universal Truth.

You will never learn to truly love
until, naked, you stand before one another in
total acceptance and trust.

A great lesson surely, humble human.

Wanderers parting glassy veils,
Keeping unto yourselves is a dying thing.
Cannot your beings feel the pain of your loneliness?
Surely one has no more or less to hide
from that of another.

Chapter 7

ALL ESSAYS ARE FROM PALPAE

ESSAY I

Fear-based decisions made among your government officials have settled the structural components of your planet into a mode of expectant negativity. In an effort to offset the alarming nature of these features, you who increasingly strain to place the full measure of your lives into proper perspective (as appropriate to soul-spirit evolution) serve as energy vessels that ease, stabilize, and counterbalance disharmonic tones. Those dedicated to pursuing Love's greater purpose aid the star tribes in alleviating potentially destructive stressors that are constantly building and settling into the vibratory fields of Earth's magnetic poles.

Western people (in the present century in particular) increasingly view as critical to life's essentials the individual's right to maintain vast arrays of possessions. However, the accumulation of these goods accomplishes little else than to ensure the entrenchment of pseudo-influential persons who wield the batons of financial and political power. The increased tempo by which they maneuver is nothing more than an abusive and corrupt attempt to maintain a facade of inherent right to manipulate and control others. However, the energy generated by the radiating lights of awakening humanity counterbalances that of the negative forces. As spiritual seekers progress, their internal lights constantly refine. Because of the dynamics involved in effecting a planet's vibrational evolution, amperage output of positively focused humans swirls ever-expanding beams of humming lights about Earth's surface, which serves to enhance the nature of our work as we go about the business of negative-wattage transfer.

Understand, the ability to harness and use Love's power is the true test of spiritual maturity. Love's energies are transmitted whenever a firm resolve is made to live in accordance with Universal Law, not by those who would assume a position of false authority over others.

We have resources available that enable us to absorb abrupt flares of energy that newly awakened persons emit whenever they suddenly transcend their baser emotions and allow a powerful ray of Light-Love to shine through them. These radiations are exceedingly raw. Therefore, they must be subdued and excess flux softly transmuted. Whenever energies of high magnitude (whether positive or negative) are suddenly broadcast into the spatial waves, we gather them within starship crystalline banks and beam them to the Pleiadian star system. There, unstable light is filtered and diffused through gigantic crystal silos, a process that could be likened to cleansing the colors of a rainbow. Brilliant hue reestablished, enhanced beams are transmitted back to the starships. Then soothed light essence is allowed to fall like gentle rain upon Earth to aid in the reconstruction of the planetary grids.

ESSAY 2

We who glide among the stars do not thoroughly understand the many ordeals that humans choose to subject themselves to. The shallow moldings upon which their multitudinous societies are erected (and of which they are inordinately proud) lack certain essentials that are basic to balanced, harmonious living. An approach to life that recognizes all its parts must function in agreement with Universal Law in ordered, peaceful coexistence with all nature's elements. We, of course, have the greatest compassion for that which limits humans' cosmic perception—manufactured articles to which they have enslaved themselves and of which they are so enamored, such as ungainly artifacts that puke clouds of black noxious materials; stuffy, grease-clogged cooking rooms; pieces of apparel that pull and tug at their freedom. We view such unpleasantries as superfluous to life. Furthermore, it is within the current state of human technological know-how to provide a much finer scenario in which they may act out the dramas of their lives.

Does the process of accumulating an abundant array of objects, the enjoyment of which you have hoped might aid you to achieve some degree of satisfaction, distract you from attending to your spiritual needs? Does this situation not cause you to feel physically stagnant and emotionally strangled? Why do you slave so at your daily tasks, the dislike of which so often causes you to weep, in order to bestow more and more objectionable articles about your person? For such do you fight, maim, and kill one another, for the "freedom" to live separated and alone in a dangerous boxlike dwelling.

Would you not rather dwell as if you lived in a field of perpetually blooming flowers? Would you not rather experience the cosmos as if it were an element of your own Oneness? Brothers and sisters, you have taken great liberties with your planetary home, which was created as an Eden and entrusted to your hands with resources and abilities within your talents to raise magnificent cities upon the lands. Instead, you degrade your soul dreams, fashioning images of buildings that resemble stiff cardboard cutouts within which you raise weak voices in a falsetto of thanksgiving. Lost opportunities have cast you into molded lives that deplete your spiritual energies and cause you much personal and collective grief.

Though you endeavor to maintain a generalized ignorance that extraterrestrials exist, we persist in loving your lights much more than you would suppose. At any rate, our presence is not obvious. We do not dwell conveniently under eyes that prefer pointing to the ground refusing to see little else, let alone inhabitants of the universes.

However, many of you struggle to awaken from your spiritual comas. May you freely absorb the details of this manuscript, allowing them to fall upon the soft places within your minds' imagery where wood ferns bend to meet tranquility's gurgling brooks. May these lines unfold peacefully before you, enrapturing your emotions. May the presence of the Star Maker and the universal beings become as one with your perception of reality. Remember, you are never separated from Creation's vibrancy except by acts of your free will.

May you place your trust, freely given, in God, also unto we who hover. Look! There in the clouded sky! Is that a starship? Indeed!

Essay 3

Time and time again, humans make most difficult for themselves what is meant to be profoundly simple. Because of their unbridled passionate natures and the generalized instability of their collective emotional state, their energy fields are severely misaligned. As a result, the joyful interlude that physical life is meant to be has deteriorated into little more than one tumultuous happening following quickly upon the heels of another. After centuries of accumulated residue from this sort of behavior, "modern" electronic media incessantly postulate upon one crisis after another, of which the ancients severely warned. The future will see the human family looking back upon these difficult years and greatly wondering at the overall laxness of twentieth-century humans to develop an abiding interest in matters pertaining to inter-galactic participation and planetary evolution.

Within the human family there is a dilemma that must be resolved. Before your planet is granted inter-galactic status, it is mandatory that you begin to think and act in resonant cohesiveness. Artificial boundaries that place a variety of countries upon the world map are severely limiting. They create an atmosphere of divided nationalism—a spiritually dangerous environment—and make it virtually impossible for the people as a whole to step upon a path of cosmic unity.

The failure of humanity to achieve solidarity is in direct defiance of the Law of One. The Absolute did not give Earth to humanity as a perpetual Eden just to have it classified into sections and colors upon parchment for any segment of people to set itself apart. By so doing, an unnatural condition has been fashioned in which pri-mary interests have become geared to the enticements of the material plane. Thus, even the most spiritually adept are virtually incapable of coming to any clear under-standing of the precepts of Original Law. We must gruffly admonish you: You cannot advance to a state of evolved grace or become accepted for knowledgeable member-ship in the great star councils by continuing your oddly infantile games.

We urgently implore you to seek greater understanding of your complex social and environmental problems. We urgently recommend that you create a more evolved approach to that which seriously challenges you.

We realize that these are very difficult matters. Solutions will not easily be put into practice by beings who are virtually comatose. The Law of Free Endeavor grants you the right to create chaos or order, a gentle approach or a rocky approach. However, what is to be will most assuredly come to be. It is in your favor that, as you become cognitive of the presence of extraterrestrial beings in residence on Earth, you will become progressively more agreeable to our suggested alterations and modifications.

Entities representing Earth—those granted seats upon the star councils—will be duly appointed by the celestially aligned governing body assigned to monitor the evolution of your solar system. You may find yourselves surprised as to the identities and forms of those selected. It will do you no appreciable benefit to flounder about like fishes upon a beach striving for individual recognition. Decision in these matters is predicated upon the integrity, life-purpose commitment, and willingness to dedicate one's energies in surrender to greater good—in other words, upon the attunement of specified beings to the harmonic coordinates of the galactic hum.

People of Earth, you have serious business to attend to. We suggest you diligently embark upon a course to massively overhaul your societal structures before they crumble and fall by the sheer weight of their over-burdened beams. Our nature is not to be harsh toward ones for whom our love is duly displayed. We do propose, however, that you prepare yourselves to willingly and openly peruse the printed materials contained within this instructional guide.

On Roads and Architecture

Beings, we congratulate you who take it upon yourselves to venture bravely within your vehicular structures to travel upon your dangerously antiquated system of roadway interchanges. You may, as an exercise in observation, prepare yourselves to notice patterns of depleted energy as your transporting device passes under bridges. The hot-cold-hot exchange that takes place is not entirely because of the sun's abrupt absence. Processing of Earth's rocky formations through grinding, mashing, heating, and pounding to lay asphalt and concrete crushes the life force out of natural geologic essences. As manufactured substances are laid upon Earth, they create zones wherein rocks' life and warmth have been thoroughly bled. You may be so inclined as to find this information of particular interest.

Architecture is, of course, the planning and construction of boxes and bowls for the containment of various life energies, for humans, animals, plants, and even geologic-based beings. The hum of artificially formed domiciles may be either uplifting to the harmonic vibrations of their inhabitants or of quality that steadily declines in magnitude as the building ages.

Any artificially formed edifice has the potential of enslaving the wills of those who reside within its walls. The essence hum of a residence is initially established through the medium of its focused patterns: its contours, the materials used in its construction, and the attitude of its builders. A circular, pyramidal, or octagonal creation is more honorable to the substance out of which its base tissue was formulated and allows processed rocks, trees, and the like to uplift the spirit of beings living within them, as if they lived among flowers and moonbeams. Conversely, the sharp-angled corners of rectangles and oblongs warp the natural flow of vibrational energy, and a less uplifting melody is hummed within their walls. This is particularly true when substances used in molding the structure are made of elements that have been unnaturally deprived of their life force without their permission and without honor, a situation common to human society. To live and work in an environment created out of materials ripped from Earth without due respect for the integrity of life force or individual will lessens the possibility that beings residing in a building so constructed will receive physical, emotional, or spiritual sustenance from their living quarters ("quarters" defined as the fourth of a whole).

For example: When an animal is housed against its will in a cage fashioned out of concrete and steel, not only is the creature denied its natural instinct for unlimited motion, but its spiritual essence is placed in jeopardy. For all intents and purposes, the animal therein is dead, though its body parts continue to function. Robbed of its right to range freely in its home environment, the animal is additionally tormented by pockets of stagnating energy that deflect downward and sideways, from wall to wall and from ceiling to floor. Trapped within the shelters used for residential and busy-ness activities, the human creature is also subject to unnatural resonations that emanate from improperly encased space.

In these pioneering years, many humans are cosmically inspired to perfect designs that will blossom as the flower-laden domiciles of the future. These men and women have come to a clear understanding that an evolved approach to designing habitats is predicated upon a spiritually mature adaptation not only of building space and materials but also of the use of pigments in harmony with the waves of energy emitted by color.

To further aid your growing awareness of these matters, sit in a quiet, meditative mode and bring your mind's eye to focus upon a clear view of the Blue Crystal Planet of the Arcturian sun system. Upon this world (which serves the galactic family as a coordinating center) massive crystals are grouped systematically and abundantly about the land. Resembling the giant silos used upon Earth for grain storage, tall, cylindrical-shaped crystals are the primary source of our "fuel supply." Inhabitants take naught from the integrity of the crystalline structures, nor do they deplete the environment; energy is sustained within the structures by nothing more than the force of thought as directed from the planet's group mind.

Circles of energy that enwrap Earth are like endless tides washing upon the oceans' shores, energy kept in motion by a force that integrates and blends regenerative waves within the planetary body. However, arising steadily from their self-created predicaments, humans' disharmonious emotional states constantly feed into the planetary vibrational grids. Humans are a primary cause of the escalating degree and variety of Earth's stressors, particularly those humans living in cities who long since have disassociated themselves from connecting in any real way with Earth or from understanding that Earth, as a living being, is basic to that which nourishes and sustains the rhythms of their life's blood.

Planetary energies are perpetually in flux, their intensities constantly rising and falling. If people are not elastic enough to bend and move as do grasses brushed by winds, they become like faults in the ground that have been riveted in one position for a very long time. Eventually, as it will always be when enough energy has been accumulated, the tension within an entity will reach a state of climactic crisis, and the strata underlying the situation must rearrange itself to ease and relieve intolerable strain. The moment maximum stress is reached and the pent-up energies are released, people who have lost their resiliency will shatter internally and will commence breaking up like a great building whose walls are tumbling about. Compare this to a quake that stirs the rocky confines of Planetary Mother.

To aid Earth in releasing pent-up pressures, the clouded starships, in cooperation with the Spiritual Hierarchy, sweep beams of vibrating colored lights into her ground and water to aid in her preparations for transcendence to harmonious alignment with the more subtle planetary and solar hums. Simultaneously, in league with Earth, many humans are themselves undergoing a process of cellular-pattern reconstruction.

Conversely, many are becoming demonstrably less capable of fulfilling the overall details of their prebirth contracts and are essentially wasting away personal power by giving over responsibility for their life decisions into the hands of others. By so doing, they place themselves into positions of being mere spectators to the dynamics of the physical world instead of being her companion creators. Thus, the possibility is very real that those beings in their next lives will discover that their DNA matrices have taken up residence in humans who closely resemble their previous lives' situations. In addition, culturally misaligned humans acting within family, work-related, or governmental units who coarsely opt to take away free will and vital forces of others (thus depriving them of a portion of their life-forming substance) predicate the placement of their own vibrational tones to more primitive, base-harmonic levels. Though humans generally consider animal and plant forms beneath them in capability, intellect, and soul-spirit connection, the cells of these wild nonhuman forms are well on their way to singing in accordance with tones of Earth-refining vibrations.

It may serve your interest to carefully consider the foregoing. To put aside matters contained within these discussions as barely deserving notice would be self-defeating. Such an attitude will only widen the growing division between you and those who yearn for the subdued ecstasy that comes when one's heart-mind is in alignment with prime harmony.

Details of Earth's structural plates are beginning to resonate in closer harmonic attunement with that which is magnificent cosmos. Though the foregoing statement may be incomprehensible, it lessens not its validity. Human science has not yet arrived to the point of viewing matter as an extension of spirit, nor does it realize that even the atoms that make up the base matter of any planetary system continuously and progressively urge themselves to align in an ever-refining degree with that which sings in complete Oneness, that is, to realize soul destination, Central Sun, Celestial Home.

Not wishing to be supportive of such informative data, government and scientific representatives throughout your world have developed certain energy patterns that exude waves of negativity into Earth's grid structures, such as in areas where chemical pollutants and nuclear waste are stored. Intellectually and emotionally refusing to represent their people as potentially vital spiritual lights, they emit certain destructive patterns that subsequently flow into Earth's energy-field grids. Although they are acting in a fashion that cultural history deems socially acceptable, the negativity which emanates from such behavior is potentially destructive to Earth. (Discordant, abrasive traits have never aligned with the naturally peaceful state of Earth Mother.) Thus, the largest and most erratic wave-producing cities—your major population centers in all countries—are carefully arranged about the planetary ball.

A fine-tuning of yin and yang energies is critical to any healthy third-dimensional entity, yet it is completely out of balance in humans who prefer cosmic sleep to enlightened awareness. The former live in a more or less constant state of spiritual disorientation, producing waves of vibrating energies in direct opposition to Love-Light harmonics. Thought patterns transmit outwardly from the brains of these negative people, forming pockets of abrasive sound that stretch along the planetary grids from polar cap to polar cap. Round and round they go, creating weblike ethereal energy fibers that resonate dissonant tones.

In an effort to readjust the staticlike sounds that could overwhelm and consume the frequencies of your vibrationally refining planet, awakening animals and humans in ever greater number are easing their internal lights to become one with the planetary grids. Merging their mutual heart-heat to flow like cords within an electrical conduit, these awesome individuals are constantly motivated to transform destructive components emitted by the thoughts of less attentive beings. They seek to align Earth's grid flows to sing in equitable fashion with harmonics hummed throughout the galaxy.

Though seemingly contradictory, the intensity of potentially volatile thought generated by disruptive influences is so strong that its wattage actually enhances the ability of this diverse band of animals and humans to move with ever-increasing rapidity from point to point along their assigned grids. By carefully maneuvering components of negative thought and in accordance with directives issued by the Regency star council, awakened animals and humans and beings of light swim, slither, walk, run, and fly streams of light outwardly along the planetary grids. Radiating high energy activated by their dedication to serve Spirit, such beings emit tones that are capable of transforming negative energy into the positive harmonics endemic of the color and sound spectrum Love-Light. Remember: Every individual, heart-mind properly attuned, has the ability to participate with the reconstructive process underway in accordance with the greater plan.

In spite of the trend for government officials world-wide to attempt a massive cover-up of any evidence that points to the presence of the intergalactic fleet, this generation's children are fast becoming aware of our visit and the purpose behind it. As Earth's vibrations continue to refine, adults will become more and more at ease with us as they, too, gain the openness of mind necessary to discern the flowered, poppy-shaped clouds that announce a gathering of the Intergalactic Brotherhood's starships.

Chapter 8

On Plants and Animals

Essay i

Tashaba

Catlike in form, like a sister is Tashaba with Patricia, she who contains essence energies that resonate in service to Spirit in the dual capacity of nature healer and star writer-scribe. For some time before she was summoned to appear before the Regency star council in the summer of 1987, Patricia, full of her brand of spiritual passion, had been dedicated to aid in the transmutation of certain pervasive, fearful attitudes that threatened the continued existence of wolves. In so doing, she managed to remove much suspicion that had covered the eyes and ears of many and helped in efforts underway to create a better understanding of this much maligned creature. Her sorrow for the plight of the endangered animal, indeed the heartfelt ache of anyone who is deeply concerned for the world's diminishing species, arose from a core of deep frustration at the lack of will shown by those "in charge" to carry their share of the burden of responsibility to avert worldwide planetary disaster.

Mirroring the ingrained disharmonic attitudes of your planet's most powerful governing bodies, the media compound the situation as they manipulate and encourage circulation of information that serves nothing more profound than to stimulate negative responses. Entrepreneurs of the news recognize and feed upon a strange perversity within humans that revels in indulging themselves in unfortunate events which destroy the lives of others.

I digress; the environmental situation is to be the key focus of this dialogue.

Seldom have humans' laws given consideration to the habitat requirements of creatures nonhuman. It is fallacious to believe any real measures have yet been implemented that contain the potential to offset the escalating problem of species' extinction. It is so critical that only a concerted effort by all humankind to rethink and reestablish behavioral boundaries can hope to effectively stave off impending disaster.

Receptive, awakening members of the human family have already begun to realize that it is their personal and collective responsibility to call upon the galactic family for assistance in overcoming their environmental difficulties. You who despair over the state of your planet's environment feel helpless and alone in your concern for her. Call upon us! We tell you, you are not alone! As we receive permission, we are able to purposefully interact with you in a direct, cooperative manner to accomplish a mutually recognized goal. In the meantime, we content ourselves by transporting and storing the genetic matrix of more willing segments of Earth's population: animals and plants threatened with planetary extinction. As they arrive, their DNA codes are placed into crystalline energy pods located upon starships and within etheric pyramids on Earth. The light essences of transported animals and plants await future restoration. Either they will return to Earth or they will be relocated to more appropriate star systems. Memory facets intact, these entities only sleep. Therefore, humans who design and launch programs to reestablish endangered species or implement chromosomal storage facilities for "extinct" species are duplicating procedures already in effect upon the zoo, or ark, ships.

Earth people, a dark state of despair rises to the surface whenever you contemplate the futility of your ability to reverse the slide into extinction that faces a great multitude of plants and animals. Many feel overwhelmed before the mechanisms that humanity's doings have set in motion. They sense that there is no way to halt the tragedy, no place to deeply breathe clear air or to drink clean water, no place that remains where they may enjoy a peaceful moment of natural solitude.

Those who devote their lifeblood in feeble attempts to protect their vanishing cousins greatly hope that by the very act of expressing love manifested as action their works will ultimately reverse the insidious trend. Voices and pens raised in protest, their words die like brambles in a brush fire before the chaotic backlash of nature thrashing about in mortal agony. Writing reams of documents and speaking out until the hoarseness of their throats overcomes their senses, these courageous people are continuously confronted by the dead will of the flippantly arrogant and the blinded eyes of those who refuse to see. All the noisy things that humans call "holy"—rockets and their red glare—are but the ungainly toys of a species who, like spoiled children, prefer to run and play undisturbed by the growing proliferation of their accumulated waste.

Historically assigned the position of principal agents in charge of protecting Earth's natural elements, humans early on reneged on their galactic contract. They overtly failed to carry out, in a discriminating and enlightened manner, their greater cosmic duties. Depending upon the course of humanity's collective choice, the genetic codes of all nonhuman life forms could be temporarily or even permanently transported to other worlds.

In a very real sense, our zoo ships are not unlike Noah's Ark, a symbol of what may yet transpire if humans refuse to humble themselves to achieve a state of conscious Oneness with animals and plants. I serve upon such a ship where Earth's precious treasures are safely stored and diligently protected.

ESSAY 2

PALPAE

Do you ponder at times as to the nature of the lives of animals whose bodies are incarcerated in cages in zoos? For animals to be placed inside confining structures is to have their life experiences devalued until they deteriorate into naught but eating and sleeping, with continuous observations by beings with little or no understanding of their perilous state. Though the imprisoned animals most often lie about in dormant postures or pace to and fro to release the energies of nervous frustration, their dominant attitude suggests a submission to fate. The reality, however, is that they only prolong lives of abject misery and delay the release that death brings. Blessed are these beings as their essence spirits are gathered into more merciful realms.

In a sense, starship inhabitants are not obligated to facilitate the transfer of entities that humans have kept locked within prisonlike environments. However, it is a special, personal joy to be of service to those forlorn creatures, for they are greatly beloved among us.

Do not suppose that you are the only beings whom we recognize as members of our galactic family. All categories of life are equal with that of One within the lineage of the star tribes. Consider well: As you imperil and imprison creatures who were meant to be freedom-born, thus do you to your own.

It would seem time to critically contemplate thought patterns that species *Homo* accepts as God-inspired. Overall, humanity has demonstrably failed to interact maturely, gracefully, and in a loving manner with the plants and animals with whom it shares planetary living space. To set forth that humanity is superior and is the only living being the Creator endowed with soul or established boundaries of extraordinary intelligence is not only gravely erroneous but presumptively arrogant as well. On a cosmic level, there is no criterion by which one species or individual is classified as exceptional in any degree over that of another.

ESSAY 3

TASHABA

Stands of trees bowing before winds that blow over the many continents are dependent upon the good will of humans to take notice of their predicament. They are prime nutrient-bearers for maintaining a balanced harmonic hum in perpetuity, and they are becoming gravely misaligned. The giants topple rapidly, yes, very rapidly. As the environment deteriorates and as the doings of humans release more and more toxic particles into the once-fragrant air, the ability of Earth's plant population to aid in cleansing the precious gases that surround her lessens. The noble and somber countenances of the majestic trees and their smaller plant cousins diminish not only in number but in variety as well. Though widely dispersed, plant entities are nevertheless absorbing poisonous materials at an alarming rate. Nature's ability to produce adequate energy allotments to sustain them dwindles as industrial pollutants permeate ever farther into the vast reaches of the globe.

Despair not, oh weak of heart, as threatened plants become progressively incapable of sustaining themselves. As is true with their animal cousins, plants' genetic codes are being stored upon the starships. There the cellular membranes of individual plants settle into a state of suspended animation to patiently await the time for reestablishment upon a world grown healthier.

Comfortably incorporating images that tumble through your thoughts as you read may help to involve you actively in the greater plan. From this day forward, may the small frustrations that haunt your life be put aside as one does the seeds of figs, as nothing more than minute bits of inconvenience. As you become aware that you can gaze upon banks of clouds and easily discern when a display of starships is hovering there, you may also be as gently attentive to the humming voice that is the song of your spirit. A very fine melody indeed!

This entity, Tashaba, is my sister Manitu's golden-maned companion. May all who come upon this message come to understand that the love we hold for humanity runs deep and is gifted to each of you individually. As you read, may waves of greater understanding wash over you like surging oceanic waters breaking over sandy shores.

May knowledge so gained cause the happenstance of your lives to strum like a cord upon a harp played by angels.

Essay 4

Tashaba

Energies that swirl, engulf, and merge into the rocky continental plates and into the vast distances that make up the oceans and the air link thoughts that constantly emanate from land-, air-, and water-based life forms. Unrestricted by the subtle boundaries humans place upon the cerebral cortexes of their own capable brains, dolphins, porpoises, and whales swim thought-free, hosts of some of the most evolved minds on your planet. These water-based mammals are constantly sending telepathic images to their land-based cousins as they patiently endeavor to open the portals of the closed human mind.

No others share in equal degree the tasks for planetary maintenance as do humans, dolphins, porpoises, and whales. The water-based mammals are primarily engaged in sustaining and healing gridlines, those interconnecting weblike patterns of light basic to the underlying energy components that make up the etheric structure of Earth Mother. They are in great need of human assistance to carry out the finer details of their evolution-enhancing work.

As the sun and moon sing whispered songs to connect solar winds to the waters and lands, may you also become attuned to the dance of mental communication that joins your thoughts with those of the elegant sea creatures. As your consciousness elevates, may you gain a greater appreciation for the special relationship between humans and sea mammals. May you assume an attitude of abundant cooperation as you learn to create an alliance of Oneness in service with other life forms.

As you shoulder your responsibilities, allocation of planetary "household" chores will be more equitably shared. The burdens the magnificent ocean creatures have borne will be dramatically lightened.

147

Chapter 9

On Earth and Humans

Essay i

Palpae

Humanity stands delicately poised before a vast precipice. Earth is about to enter the yawning portals of an energy window that is ready to lure it into the resonating hum of fifth-dimensional domains. We are attempting to entice humans to create a mass energy of common-based consciousness and to proceed to a state of Oneness in order to collectively merge with Planetary Mother as she takes her unprecedented step. We must also persuade humans to seriously consider putting to rest all activities that tamper with the rhythmic harmonies of the natural world.

As a whole we find you slow to awaken. Most of you remain blithely ignorant as to the intricacies of planetary and species evolution, though indicators of change surround and flow about you as persistently as do dust motes dancing in a ray of sunlight.

Greatly intrigued with the fascination and busy-ness of dividing the world's continents into specific geographic sections, humans perpetuate the illusion that one being or a particular set of beings has the God-given prerogative to hold sway over others or to control and gather to themselves that which they view as rightfully theirs. As documented historically, the ideologies of "sophisticated" men and women became focused upon the energies that drive their physical desires. The motivation to accumulate as much property and material goods as possible resulted directly from this mode of thinking. Human society, built upon the premise that what one is in possession of is "one's own," agrees that it is more or less permissible to accumulate further for oneself what others call "their own," if one has the ability to successfully manipulate them out of their treasure troves of collected goods. Deluded by the doings of their busy brains, humans have forgotten that Creator did not manifest your beautiful planet for the pleasure of a few to horde as a source of political, economic, or religious wealth and power.

"Civilized" people, left to their own devices, like unsupervised children play freely with the properties of will, ignoring the ramifications of the Law of Cause and Effect. Appointed your world's prime caretaker, humanity's collective responsibility is to respect Earth, to love her, to gently tend to her as one would an elderly and beloved mother in order to rebirth humanity's ancient relationship within the greater cosmic family. It is indeed unfortunate that the bulk of the responsibility for maintaining the health of your planet fell to animals and "primitives" because the desire for conquest overcame the good sense of the majority. That which once was in harmony between humans and nature degenerated into nothing more than a means to sustain the illusions of a population otherwise engaged in amusing itself with a set formula of antagonistic interspecies hostility.

It has become a complicated thing to live gracefully upon Earth. Only very, very few remain more or less cognizant of the soul resonations upon which individuals' relationships to their friends and families are built, let alone to that of cows solemnly munching in grassy fields or water flowing over stones in gurgling brooks. You are now faced with your greatest challenge: to put aside all shortsighted self-indulgence and take your place as fully functioning members of the greater galactic community.

The words in these essays may prove to be too much for many to bear. It may please you to turn your backs upon what is not pleasurable. Prior to so doing, however, we suggest that you closely investigate all aspects of your physical reality. Consider the volatile state of your society and the decaying condition of your major cities. Ponder the instability of your system of monetary exchange. Observe, if you will, the water and air. Consider: If you could communicate with the animals and plants, what would they share of the love they bear for a species that murders them and makes slaves of their will in order to bend them to yours? Did you neglect to ask of Creator permission to dig, poke, push, pull, stamp upon, kill, or cut and burn what was designed for the needs and pleasures of all your planet's creatures?

In addition to the depressed health of biological forms, it may interest you to consider what is essential to geologic life: gold, silver, precious metals, gemstones, and the like. Priceless are these commodities, yet these entities, like their animal and plant cousins, are becoming increasingly rarified in their natural habitats and are not undeserving of being classified as endangered species. The very act of ripping rocky substances from the ground demolishes the viability of their life-force energies. Metals, gemstones, and such, though seemingly small in relation to the huge bulk of Planet Mother, nevertheless are vital to the stability of her overall well-being. Humans' obsession with removing all veins of gems, metals, and pockets of oil and gas for their exclusive use is seriously depleting the harmonic hums of the continental plates.

As you advance to the time for taking your seats upon the star councils, the dormant abilities of your now-slumbering minds will greatly expand. Newly proficient, brains fully activated, you will be able to focus the full thrust of your minds so that the force of generated thought will become Earth's primary power source. As Earth moves into her fifth-dimensional slot, giant crystals will serve as your main, nondepleting fuel source. The clear song of pristine light that crystalline structures emanate will be effortlessly used and as effortlessly restored.

Earth will no longer sustain humanity's insensitive meddling with the structures of her exterior body. We suggest that this remark be taken as one whose undertones hum with a sense of utmost urgency.

ESSAY 2

PALPAE

Closely observe hovering banks of clouds as they settle comfortably about distant horizons. Hark to their whispers, for your instincts are wise and your subconscious minds know that what blows interminably through the straits of the airy oceans contains images of starships riding gracefully upon gentle undulations of flowing winds. We who reside aboard the starry crafts request that you openly consider these essays, for we have carefully spread their sweet tones upon these sheets of paper.

Essays pertinent to this volume will be transmitted, in one form or another, over and over and over again until their energies settle comfortably into the farthest recesses of your awakening minds, until they reach into the very core of your being. The epoch of unevolved humanity, the time in which one species demands the right to dominate and control other life forms (including its own), is coming to an end.

We suggest that humans maneuver themselves into position to institute a massive transformation of the bulky foundations of temporal society. Energies that have historically sustained your institutions are rapidly diminishing in vigor. Artificial sounds that resonate from the synthetic-filled edifices of your most renowned cities have become increasingly subdued as the vibrations of their harmonic pitch are lowered by the sorrowful emotions of beings residing there. Few remain long enticed to prolong their stay in such places, except the abjectly lonely and disheartened. Only the homeless and unemployed persistently linger, their forlorn cries merging with the stones of forgotten and decaying buildings.

The metropolises of which you are so proud function mainly as repositories for drudging work and frenzied pleasures. As the attractions of such things quickly pale, those who indulge in their enticements scurry away (when able) to more pleasant suburban areas, where they earnestly hope to find some degree of solitude and inner peace. The vast urban regions cannot sustain a constant state of negative intonations for an indefinite time. The structures within the largest cities are in imminent danger of collapse, of toppling like so many unbalanced and overburdened blocks. Do not delay. The time has come to put your house in order!

Essay 3

Palpae

Softly, night falls upon your slumbering planet. Earth Mother hums her song, for she honors the sacredness of her natural rhythms. The makeup of her greater bodily substance, the rocky layers, though eternally whittled away by the elements, is never lost, but regroups as minute granules of sand. Like processes of erosion that transform the most resistant granite into the finest of sandy flakes, time's rigid essence is rapidly extricating its delicate fibers from the restricted layers of the physical plane. Hereafter, time will rise and fall ever more naturally, like flowing streams of clear water.

The winters of your discontent are nearly played out. Spring, summer, and fall—the seasons of historical humanity—fade, becoming nothing more than fleeting memories, brief reflections of a forgotten past. Harsh, that which was prophesied transpires. Like a pall, the events of the times settle upon you. Frightened at these strange events, you struggle to maintain the status quo. Nevertheless, the illusionary substance of the third-dimensional plane, in which you barely function, will continue to dissolve as your planet submits to the processes of cosmic rebirth. The massive continental plates rumble and quake. Unleashed, nature's energies—water, fire, and wind—escalate in intensity as Earth Mother cleanses herself in preparation for the transformation of her cellular mass into higher octave dimensions.

Eternally, the breezes blow. Vastly rich, the season's crops bend in rhythm with the cutting blades as lush fruits, peas, beans, and grains are diligently gathered and carefully secreted in cellars and storage bins in preparation for the austere months that lie ahead. Chaff, left behind to rot in snowy fields, nevertheless remains. Before spring planting, the residue must be properly removed.

Resembling the shuckings of more productive products, nuclear waste also lies buried in the ground, blissfully and irresponsibly ignored, a horror ready to explode upon a self-deluding society. The waters of the once-pristine oceans are cluttered with stagnant flakes and mounds of foul, reeking garbage. Abominable, plastic falls like leaves from deadened trees upon the creatures that make the seas their home. Like maggots crawling over sludge, the plastic floats, deadly traps set to capture the innocently unwary.

Humankind, what is your plan to correct these atrocities?

We who monitor are cognizant that we feed you a bitter pill. We are not unaware of your growing desire to set right what you have inadvertently created. We are not unaware that you did not set out in a deliberate fashion to foul your own nest. Although there have always been men and women who intentionally and imprudently gather for their selfish uses all the resources they can possibly muster, in reality they number but a few. The majority would rather shine like lights with nature's garments flowing gracefully about them, if only they had not lost the ability to plunge gaily and freely into the pure waters of their once-virtuous hearts.

Do not feel dismayed if you perceive that your role in these things seems inconsequential. Be diligent about that which is yours to do. Each morn, as the sun beckons you to arise to a new day, be consciously attentive to the sweet whispers that urge you to be consistently true to your Self's profound calling. As you startle your heart into fulfilling its grandest passion, your soul harmonics will settle into a perfectly pitched rhythm. Then you will dynamically and effectively serve in cooperative alliance with that portion of humanity who is in a state of perfect at-one-ment with the hum of Earth Mother.

We bid you a softness.

ESSAY 4

ARCTURIAN STAR COUNCIL

Be attentive; the following is of the utmost importance.

Do you find yourself too busy with life's chores to carefully assimilate these data? "No time, no time!" Like the rabbit that runs about with the girl and the teapot, do you scatter, scatter? Like old brown leaves brushed aside by the winds of winter, does your attention easily flutter about? Pay heed! Critical matters are at hand. Your planet no longer sleeps. The mother ship rides closely to the day when her full-bodied form will slide into the transpositional slot of the fifth-dimensional state.

Yes, like a ship is Earth, bounding along upon the cascading seas of unrelenting space. Onward she goes, and you with her, riding uneasily upon her back like a mote of dust upon the carcass of a dying whale.

As a whole, humankind, you have blotted the once-pristine beauty of your exquisite planet. You sneeze germs of self-indulgence upon her delicate skin. You hunt her creatures and you soil her water and air. You dig into her bosom and extricate her finest jewels. You mash her, refine her, and grind her delicate parts into flakes and powders from which to manufacture more and more goods in the hopes of satiating your insatiable desires. You strike fear into the innocent. With knives, guns, traps, and poisons you decimate the children of your aching planet.

Do no comforting remarks emanate from the bowels of this essay? Indeed, none seem at hand. If you are to find consolation for such doings, you must turn inward and honestly and thoroughly examine your degree of participation in these grave doings. Have you attempted, to the best of your ability, to live in such a way that your actions speak loudly of your intention to serve as an example of the importance of living in harmony with the natural elements of your planetary home?

Do you feel some sense of trepidation as to the method of "Judgment Day" processing? We do not intimate that the time will come when face-to-face you will be required to explain yourself to a devil before an oven or an angel upon a cloud. However, ask yourself if you always attempt to shine brightly as a being human. Do you maintain a compassionate composure when faced with the sorrows and difficulties of others? Do you move through the grandeur of your life with, at the very least, a determined resolve to approach your day's events with an attitude that reflects high spiritual integrity?

We hum as One. Committed in service to Earth planet, solar quadrant Sol, it is our unfortunate responsibility to pronounce mind-thoughts that are outlined in this essay. Be not unaware that the state of Earth is very critical to the interests of the galactic core.

159

ADDENDUM: MESSAGE FROM SANANDA

It is neither sacrilege to seek a new religion nor blasphemy to contemplate the Christed energy as a being of magnificent light. What is evil, truly evil, is to deny or obstruct another's path to spiritual enlightenment. Any religion, no matter how "great," that seeks to entrap its followers by establishing a narrow set of rules by which the priests and church elders hope to ensnare the bulk of humanity does not, and never has, served to the Good of your planet. It is further stated that the Christ was an example of the just times, the season of purity that, like a storm cleansing the ground, would one day unleash His message across the lands of Earth unto the farthest corners, to the highest mountains, and into the depths of the deepest seas.

This generation's children, of their own accord, will easily discern the immaculate wisdom upon which His profound teachings are based. These virtuous beings, cloaked in protective shields of childlike innocence, will surely see the day the starships descend. This generation's elders and those trapped in the fears and dark secrets of the worldly middle-aged will find themselves divided. Although many spiritually struggling beings will ascend to planes of perpetual rapture, a great many others will find themselves dwelling in less comfortable vibrational hums—not hell, nor even purgatory, but simply in regions that lie snugly and securely beneath the harmonies of the more ecstatic octaves. The newly formed body of Earth Mother, as she takes on the manifestations of an evolving light planet, will see a goodly number of her human population no more.

Further: The sacred tablets, the lost repositories of high knowledge, though remaining secreted within the rocky contours of your holiest lands, soon will be revealed and the ancient teachings restored. And know this as well: The caskets that held the brittle bones of the magnificent entities who once roamed the hills and valleys of Atlantis and the mother land, Mu, need not be sought after. The energies of those beings walk Earth even now, encased in the bodies of twentieth-century men and women, reborn citizens of lost continents.

Those whom kings would make into serfs are the enlightened ones, those who serve. They wash dishes, plant plants, and tend to the infirm. Their interactions with others incorporate the songs that the stars sing into the cellular mass of those around them. Their bright lights reach into the very soil and radiate into the planetary air.

They carry into the world energies of highest Love. As peals of vibrant laughter bring healing to the dis-at-ease, the shining brilliance of these beings' lives falls like seeds of magical music upon shadowed grounds. Love's unique energies become enmeshed in and emerge from clothing that bodies of the spiritually awakening wear.

The babes are wiser than the parents. The parents are wiser than the elders. The deaf grow deafer. The blind grow blinder. This is the way beings human have chosen to manifest Creation's laws.

Woe to the fallen, the mighty are arising.

Woe to those who tender money falsely, for they will not know God's house for many aeons to come.

Woe unto those who covet the mates of others.

Woe unto those who seek "justice" through war and through the warping of God's One Law, Love.

Love others even more than you love yourself; for indeed, those who love and share their bounty with one another in these magnificent days will be those who dwell in His chambers, and they will rise like the phoenix to find that their spirits need no longer take on the pseudo-trappings of a fallen race.

Woe unto those who keep cattle and lambs to be taken to the slaughter, for they will be kept as prisoners in a slough of their own making.

Woe unto those who irresponsibly wreak havoc upon the lands, those who rape for ill-gotten and selfish gains the delicate membranes of this once-exquisite planet, for as they reap, so shall they sow. They are temporarily blinded; the day is close at hand when they, too, will begin to understand what it is they have done, and a grief most profound will be theirs to endure. They will labor long and hard to overcome their pain, but peace will not be theirs for a long, long time.

Woe unto those who govern cruelly and seek to hide truth from those they were raised to serve, for they shall drown in pools of their own sorrows. Their greed is so great, their need for power is so immense, that they shall come to know well the scorching heat of the brightest sun. The desert worlds will be the places their reborn souls will inhabit, and that which is truly powerful will shine down hot and glaring upon them. In time, these unfortunate beings will come to know that their malevolent desires worshiped naught but false gods.

Though these words are harsh words, and though they may seem to tell of a God full of mighty vengeance, know by their meaning that That Which Is Profound gives unto each of Creation's children the blessing of equal opportunity and endows each culture with a teacher, an avatar supreme. What is taught by That Which Is One is none other than how to Love. Love, manifested as the driving force behind one's life, surely has the power to send Love's benefactors straight to heaven's pearly gates.

Hell is indeed a creation of the individual, for what one desires the most is soon grown. What is dark is not without promise, not without light, but only without immediate hope.

Suffer thyself to become like a child and surrender

freely into Innocence's abundant arms. Then God will gather you up and deposit you like a radiant light to shine before the thrones of the angels, for the angels do eagerly attend to those who call upon them from the purity of a childlike heart.

These tidings are not pleasant, but neither is the alternative, that which serves evil before Light. The beings who worship the Dark Lords will find themselves upon a new world, an untried world, a world much like Earth was in her beginning. It is not that the world will itself be malevolent; it is only that the physical demands of a newly forming planet are harsh and untested. Those who make the choice to live as disharmonious beings upon planet Earth predicate future lives upon a nether world.

Those who are abundant with the intention to express Light-Love seek one another out, and they *will* find one another. These enlightened beings have decreed that they will apply wisely, in manifest reality, the wisdom they have gained through their knowledge of the most sacred traditions. Recorded throughout the lands, these basic teachings stand clearly written for all to know and to shape their lives by.

These are the beginning years of the Golden Age. That which has been laid down will soon come to pass. The final chapters of your history are being brought to a close. All sorrow will fade as the new dawn is born.

From the Holiest of Holies, these words are printed.

Chapter 10

On the Evolution of Planet Earth and Humankind

Essay 1

Palpae

We, the people of the universe, salute you who prepare to surrender gracefully into the energies of the
emerging future. You are today's visionaries, the bravest
of the brave. Many of you are willing to die for what your
intellects barely understand but what your hearts freely
embrace.

The hazy veil that separates your planet from the
ethereal realms rapidly dissipates. To explain: Atomic
particles that make up the base of your planetary body are
ripe for transference to a more refined vibrational hum.
Historically, Earth has been limited by the primitive
nature of her structural makeup. That is, she has had to
adapt herself to abide by certain restrictions imposed, by
necessity, upon all third-dimensional life forms. However,

she is being closely groomed for initiation into the fourth-
and then into the fifth-dimensional range. We who monitor her progress are adjusting the pitch of her cellular
membrane to withstand transposition of her harmonics to
match that of a higher wavelength frequency. Though the
song your planet sings is something that cannot be tasted,
felt, seen, or heard within the human sensory spectrum,
we assure you, the mother sweetly resonates.

Though it may amaze you that transdimensional
beings of light are deeply immersed in processes peculiar
to planetary evolution, from our viewpoint your solar
system is not an altogether unique assignment. We grant,
however, that the influences radiating from your spatial
quadrant do present some rather unusual challenges.
Because of negative emissions constantly arising from the
average human brain, high-density, potentially destructive energy waves cover your planet like a volatile force
field. This condition must be transcended by more peaceful rays. To accomplish this feat, we are helped by humans
who serve their own and Earth's evolution by willingly
living in specific regions. The human energy body acts, in
effect, as an electrical space conduit. To this end, thousands upon thousands of alert, open-minded humans live
along critical gridlines. These spiritually attuned individuals are becoming quite adept in their roles as mission
ground crew, as light-beam-coordinating facilitators.

Preparing solar and planetary bodies for immersion
into the exceptional realms is our form of applied spiritual "work." It is a holy privilege for the team making up

the Intergalactic Brotherhood of Light. For example, it is essential that the quickening resonations of an evolving planet be kept in equal proximity with the hums emitted by other members of its solar family. Planets such as Jupiter are exceptional resources for this purpose and enhance our light and sound techniques within the system as a whole. From the depths of Jupiter we "mine" a variety of multipurpose energy rays. The spatial limits of certain beams correspond in width and length with those of barriers erected to prevent improperly tuned third-dimensional entities (solar or otherwise) from prematurely penetrating the interludes of the finely sculptured worlds.

To allow an evolving solar system to flow into the corridors of a previously established, unified fifth-dimensional celestial complex, zones within the restriction belt must first be "melted" and a window provided as sort of an escape hatch. The intergalactic team's priority task is to ensure that over- and underlying layers of an evolving system be thoroughly modified in accordance with harmonic tones of subtler dominions. It is as if the bass notes of a piano were modulated until they vibrated at the same frequency as the soprano notes.

Though bits of knowledge gleaned from the foregoing text may seem obscure to you, if you become genuinely receptive to the finer nuances of the data it will serve our mutual interests. To a certain extent, exchange of exquisite information is essential to aid densely oriented beings (such as humans) in transferring the bulk of their physical mass into that of light. To elucidate: The primary function of this intergalactic instructional manual is to incorporate, on the physical plane, a duplication of what is apparent on the ethereal planes.

Certain of our maneuvers may, of course, appear quite complicated, if considered solely from the viewpoint of system-oriented, structuralized human scientific philosophy, which tends to separate items category by category. Simplistically, one may define our interactions as light seeding. All phenomena in the manifest universes arise from the One Source, That Which Is the Creative Energy, omniscient Light-Love.

To illustrate a specific germination procedure: Sense within your visionary eye a sun that is the brightest of all suns imaginable. Such a sun is not unlike the material we have generated into Earth's internal core via a method of interweaving radiantly colored, impeccably humming beams of pure light. Our strategy is to establish certain criteria within your crystalline planetary core that, in and of itself, will aid in redefining and upgrading the nuclear density of the planetary whole. By inserting certain aspects of an evolved star's energies mid-Earth, your planet's cellular-body vibrations are enhanced a thousandfold in a vastly short, precisely determinate period of time. Correspondingly, as your planet's harmonic hum uplifts in tonal resonation, awakening humans are presented with an unprecedented evolutionary opportunity. (A human is an excellent qualifying example of a light essence that is predetermined to incarnate in a material-based body.)

Like radiating swirls of water, your evolving solar family (Earth, her sister planets, their satellites, and the sun) are being energized to cooperate as one enormous, intelligent being. Moving as an interwoven web of light, eventually they will erupt en masse upon the finely tuned galactic strands, which we describe as poppy- or rose-scented wisps.

We urge you to become increasing adept at sensing the light, sound, and color dimensions by expanding your perception of what seems to be nothing more than clouds drifting lazily through the skies. Do not be hesitant in stretching past your normal comfort zone. To exclude the possibility that starships can resemble fluffy, wispy clouds is equivalent to dismissing one's self as a living organism (that which is material) or, more to the point, an incarnated spirit.

Essay 2

Palpae

The time allotted for humans to voluntarily attend to their spiritual advancement decreases even as these words take form. Waves of flowing energy that make up the awakening collective mind substantially accelerate as an unprecedented influx of information is made widely available. Humanity's rapidly advancing computer technology is enabling both the beings of light and the Dark Lords to generate vast quantities of data via your richly diverse creative arts. The current generation is bombarded by both positive and negative visual and auditory materials. As a result, the state of nervous apprehension common to the human species in the best of times has become highly intensified, making the times extraordinarily ripe for spiritual and mental development.

Fear-based thoughts manifest tangibly as dark forms in the astral regions, so it becomes increasingly imperative for you to persevere in moving quickly through any self-defeating emotions or intellectual moods that delay you from establishing a solid, loving relationship with Prime Creator. We gently remind: Planetary and solar bodies are like sponges that easily incorporate thought forms generated by beings living upon them. To prevent potentially destructive emanations from disrupting the equilibrium of Earth's continental plates, we are endeavoring to pacify the stinging thoughts of a populace that has lived in fear of nuclear annihilation since the closing years of the second world war. Negative vibrations are flying about like maddened hornets on a rampage; we promptly transmute them before they penetrate deeply into Earth. However, they continue to circulate around the land masses, and the air and water remain subject to the often violent ebbs and flows of the characteristically anxious human temperament.

As an exercise in redefining your relationship with the forces of nature, clearly understand your personal connection with the gases that make up the planetary air. Meditate upon this etheric substance that is absolutely vital to the continuation of life as you know it. Further, consider the flux of residue from the lungs of millions and millions of beings. Visualize the impact of an essence as fragile as breath being expelled upon the magnificence of atmospheric layers. Further imagine the heavy belching of dark clouds of discordant thought that constantly pours from billions of undisciplined brains. Examine closely how your busy, worried thoughts let loose take upon themselves a devilish sort of form. Watch them scampering gleefully hither and yon like so many nasty little demons. Observe how their playful antics rip and tear at the planetary grids, how their connecting points begin to filter outward to intertwine with the deliciously scented lights of the spatial light strands. Imagine!

It is a powerful weapon, the human mind whose owner has granted it unbridled permission to impudently wander free. 'Tis our challenge to motivate you to closely monitor the passionate moods of your creative minds. It is time indeed for you as individuals and as a collective to realize that you are accountable not only for the consequences of your external behavior but also for the ramifications of your internal behavior.

The invitation to become as One with the galactic tribes is not issued to a specified minority. This starry gift is a package deal offered to the lot of you. We further challenge you to acknowledge your status as cosmic beings and to tie yourselves into a knot of Oneness that is indicative of a species harmoniously united. The times demand that you take the plunge into the swirling tides of evolution's ocean, or you will find yourselves left far behind like lonely souls stranded upon a beach. Your ability to choose otherwise is drastically diminished. Humankind, you are running out of options.

Do you wonder about the validity of so many telepathic messages descending upon Earth from extraterrestrial beings who proclaim that they travel about in hokey-poky UFOs? Indeed, this is something quite scary! Better grab the guns and shoot at those monsters before they suck out your parts. There you sit, scoffing, frightened half out of your wits. How pitiful! You and we are spirits of light. In truth, we are one entity, eternally connected by the Loving force of the One Mind. Neither one is better or lesser than the other, neither one more or less beautiful than the other. In the mind of Prime Creator, there is no integral ingredient that differentiates one being from that of another. Same! Same! Same! Identical in essence, our ethereal selves are all magnificent lights that shimmer with the most brilliant of hues!

ESSAY 3

PALPAE

Entities who cooperate in coordinating our instructions help offset the fatalistic moods that flourish Earthside. Consider: To contemplate negativism each day lessens the degree of attainment of peaceful unification with one's higher Self.

Our manipulation procedures to restructure the cellular makeup of Earth are more or less on schedule. But the primary determination for the acceleration of Earth's surface areas rests upon you, humans, and very little time remains for the completion of your duties. Time taken for surface modifications are predicated upon people committed to redefining the nature of their relationships with Earth and with Prime Creator. It has fallen to this generation to assist its star-based brethren in transforming Earth so that she can assume her proper role as an activated member of the United Federation of Planetary Affairs, Intergalactic Brotherhood of Light.

Advancement to unified interaction with beings of starry realms is not an evolutionary step for only humans, but it will incorporate all Earth-based organisms: animals, plants, rocks, water, and air. It will serve you well to perceive *all* material manifestations as essential components of vital essence, which is Prime Creator. How wondrous: There will come a point in your awakening when you will freely embrace even Earth's geologic strata as a member of your holy family.

Enmeshed, as you are, in the broiling times of transformation, you may be developing a sense that events associated with the evolutionary process are not something out of the ordinary. That which is future's course is easy to recognize if you are closely observant of the past. However, one procedure quickly follows upon the heels of another as extraordinarily powerful beams of light carefully sweep Earth's membranes clean while she becomes increasingly vibrationally realigned.

It behooves me to counsel you that a great many

spectacular things are to confront you in the years immediately ahead. Many of these doings will be most clearly
observable, for their natures will be overt. Others will be
more delicately subtle.

Your planet is exceptionally magnificent! Behold her
radiance, this wondrous entity, Earth! If you listen closely,
you will be able to discern the rhythmic melodies sung by
the winds and trees at play. You will begin to hear the
clouds hum and the weaving tapestry of grasses as they
bend and sway in ecstatic concert with summer's breezes.
Truly, the enhancement of your inner peace is predicated
upon the sight of nature's face smiling toward you.

That Which Is Omnipresent winks equally at us all
and nods at us through the blinking lights of the shimmering stars. It is the embodiment of the many suns. We
are, one and all, the vast array of God's collected children,
whatever the shape of our figures.

May you joyfully assimilate the words we have placed
before you. The hues of our essences rise brightly as we
contemplate the graceful arcs representative of the bright
lights of awakening humanity.

Essay 4

Palpae

Impatient people, you who would have starships
shining without further delay from your gardens, do you
want your way clear? Would you have us ease the road
before you with no regard as to what would become of

you without your going through what must be accomplished before such a wondrous event takes place? Nevertheless, we stand greatly compassionate of the difficult issues with which you continue to struggle. You must understand: Because of vibrational adjustment modifications to Earth's light body and the escalating numbers who are spiritually awakening, there is (and will continue to be for some time) much that will affect you personally. There are many ways we could state the reasons for this and that, yet your human minds and emotions easily stray into designs of helplessness whenever it all becomes "too much to bear."

The tightly woven cord of linear time connecting human perceptions to the past, present, and future is about to be severed. Humanity is about to face that moment when it will realize it has been summoned to present itself before the star councils. We suggest that as individuals you prepare yourselves for this great adventure by deliberately fine-tuning your emotional, mental, physical, and spiritual bodies.

We are most kindly benevolent toward you. It would fit our pleasure systems greatly to ease that which pulls and tugs at you. However, we cannot undo what you prefer to endure as the status quo. Though we are free to make suggestions and to prepare informative materials (such as this manual) to aid those who search for a greater understanding of universal affairs, it is not our place to demand that you relinquish what you prefer to retain. Divine, Absolute Intention allows no leeway for those serving the Light to preempt the responsibility each of you must take for living your life. However, those who willingly endeavor to enmesh with the conglomeration of beings who hum as one with the many stars stand tall before us.

The day will come when our tutelage of humanity will end. Then you will find yourselves fully awakened and completely revitalized. You will know that you have taken your place in harmonious unity with the vast array of entities who serve Prime Star Maker through the Intergalactic Brotherhood.

ESSAY 5

PALPAE

In mid-1987 at the time of the Harmonic Convergence, starships began to accelerate their gridline-strengthening maneuvers. Since then, refinement procedures have continued to escalate and vibrational enhancement of Earth's crystalline core has greatly improved. Earth Mother stretches and expands like an embryo about to hatch from an eggshell. She creeps ever closer toward the day of her birth as a celestial companion to the exquisitely vibrating light worlds. Thus, it becomes necessary for all plants, animals, and humans desiring simultaneous birth to transcend their embodied states and evolve with Earth as she enters the final stages of octave retoning.

Harsh, artificial lights that glare forth from your megacities are certainly not the brightest lights to penetrate the sensitive optic orbs of the star travelers. Indeed not! Like small balls of self-contained incendiary fires, arcing light beams from passionate, spiritually awakening humans blaze into the night skies. Committed to greater purpose, these numbers consciously serving the Spiritual Hierarchy grow daily. It is apparent that, in the near future, a ratio of positive radiating energies will, at long last, override the wattage power of the Dark Lords, who have long held the beings of your beautiful planet captive.

To honor the data presented in this document with an agreeable, open mind is a leap forward in trust for the average human. We are not unaware that vast numbers of this generation will never become comfortable with the information being offered for the enlightenment of the spiritually discerning. But an in-depth analysis of these materials will greet adventurous humans with the fact that these things are not particularly revolutionary. Humans do, however, require extensive maturation in the manner in which they process knowledge. Essentially, humanity's current problems are a direct result of an intelligent species agreeing to sustain itself by gorging upon juiceless morsels of rigid religious and cultural law and dry attitude tidbits steeped in a nuts-and-bolts approach to science.

Extrastellar beings assigned to live multiple lives as humans upon Earth are, in these latter years of the twentieth century, reawakening. As their light essences are refreshed, dedicated starseeds resume their duties as special emissaries to Earth from the intergalactic core.

As they realize their daily purpose is to serve Source, their inner lights begin to resonate and vibrate to a pre-established tonal code. Unaware, for the most part, that their physical forms have become miniature interspatial field resonators, these beings move about their day's activities, the light power they generate instrumental in transmuting accumulated negative-charged residue that lies upon Earth's delicate grids to positive-charged energies characteristic of a celestially healthy planet.

As a postscript, note that this essay has not been processed through investigational techniques approved by human scientific methods. Therefore, you may not agree with the essay as written. Nevertheless, we persevere and reiterate: The ability to experience one's self in the tonal range of the positive harmonics as a song expressed through the energies of Love's delicious appetite is in accordance with Prime Law. Your intense desire to serve God activates properties of Divine Love within you and energizes the vibrancy of your spirit's light.

All fifth- and sixth-dimensional Arcturians are in positive alignment with vibrational overtones of Light-Love. Individuality intact, we resonate as one massive energy field.

Essay 6

Tashaba

If you closely monitor the skies for signs of increasing starship activity, you will be exceedingly gratified. Earth herself glimmers ever so much brighter now that the melodious tones of her pulsating energies are beginning to adjust to the more delicate vibrato of the sweeter celestial hums.

As if they sing like one entity in harmony with the growing ecstasy of Planet Mother, evolving and awakening humans gently resonate, so much so that their core lights may be likened to brilliant, lacy flower petals scattered in abandon before glowing shafts of a midsummer's moon. As they become still, in blessed meditative silence, wonder of wonders the beautiful instruments of their quiescent minds begin to play the mysterious song of their souls' eternal harp. Devotional, meditative prayer is the trigger that empowers their spirits to burst forth as surging, shining rays of vibrant, spectacular light.

On the other hand, now that nights and days are quickening and the massive collective unconscious struggles with the tightening shackles of humanity's pervasive, discordant baggage, the spirit lights of the profoundly sleeping ones flicker as if they gasped for life's last breath.

Upon the starships, we are acutely aware of humanity's escalating emotional and mental torment. Though our words may fall harshly upon your sensitive ears, the intention behind them is neither to sting nor to further injure your already damaged psyches, but to activate the willing. To toss you crumbs and a false promise that only easy living lies before you would not do justice to the overwhelming gravity and magnitude of the problems your species faces. Our intention is not to cause you to run and hide from us in shame or to cause you to feel tendrils of defeat wrapping about you in a strangling fashion. We come to you in Love.

Become one with us! Trust that in transposing your limited perceptions to that of a higher reality you will do yourselves no harm. We say this: It is not necessary for any being, of any kind, to fall into a pit of self-imposed defeat. Stand instead before your mirrors and see your inner beauty shining forth. Courageously, and with great dignity, understand that hidden behind the fear that so often reflects from your beautiful faces, beneath the glazed surface of your sorrow-filled eyes, is captured a being of magnificent light. That vision, which is representative of *your* attunement (at-one-ment) to Spirit, is the point upon which you may more appropriately focus.

The complexities of a world growing daily smaller, because of the quickening of your communication networks, are like a snail dragging itself over a carpet of sand in comparison to the echoes and rebounds, the swirling and whirling of the planet's aura whenever you, in your heart-to-thought whispers, speak the hushed name of peace, of Love. Whenever you are caught in peaceful Love's brilliant trajectory, a great light bursts forth from your spirit. When your body grows weary and night's shades close slowly about, allow your head to descend upon your fluffy pillow. Offer up a simple prayer to always seek peace and practice Love. Gather together the budding blossoms of the genuine *you*. Attend strictly to your heart's warmest desires. Nourish them into magnificent being without the squeaking voice of another telling you what your gauzy dreams should be made of. Do not be hesitant in attempting to open the veil that, when drawn shut, closes your heart-mind from interacting one-to-one with beings of the starry realms.

I purr in my realization of That Which Is Absolute. I note, too, a dawning future and visualize the people human coming upon the starships. I am able to clearly see that there will come a time when we will welcome you among us. By the loving touch that is, I do embrace the universe of my birth. By the sparkling lights of the galaxy that is my home do I send my delight forth as a gift to you.

Essay 7

Palpae

It may serve your best interests to consider: We of the suns of the many planets have come forth to procure your awareness to accept That Which Is Absolute.

Further: As ordained in star council, human government and military officials are not to be allowed easy access to the buttons that are poised, ready to unleash worldwide destruction upon their planet. Upon the planet Cheuel of the Arcturian system such destruction happened. The energies of those responsible were detained upon planet Earth for millions of years, their spirits confined in order to release and purge the karma generated by disharmonious resonations abruptly unleased upon our galaxy by such an indefensible act. These beings (mostly in human form) are now awakening as if from deepest coma. They walk among you and their numbers are many.

Thus, we have come among you in the latter days of the twentieth century to reactivate the children of the planet Cheuel (and others whose origins encompass many energy-essential star systems). Inwardly they long for their lost homes. Magnificent red sun-star Arcturus was originally a system of twenty-five planets. The destroyed planet Cheuel lingers yet in the subconscious memories of the awakening starseeds.

Do not dismiss that which shines in the night sky as being merely dots of light upon a dark canvas. Many star-suns hold within the arms of their pulsating energies one or more planets whose populations are participating members of the Intergalactic Brotherhood of Light and the star councils.

I may be vibrationally identified as Palpae, Arcturian Coordinate Ambassador to Planetary System Sol. I serve to the Joint Angelic-Galactic Councils, under the auspices of the Christed energy, Sananda. Like a bolt of lightning shines His radiant essence.

Essay 8

Quoarts and Quantra

Transparent are your thoughts. To permanently dwell under the supposition that you are not capable of one-on-one acquaintance with starship personnel is a limited visualization of your own making. Generally speaking, many of you are quite consciously aware of pinpricks of telepathic waves moving subtly through your brains as we transmit thought into the heart-minds of our awakening family. Meditative, solitudinous silence is of utmost necessity for you to consciously communicate telepathically with multilevel beings. Flowing soft and gentle, like petals of a rose falling slowly to the ground upon the waves of a summer's breeze, do our thought energies connect. Thus we have oft stated, thus we repeat. We find it necessary to encourage through repetitious dialogue as we reactivate the sublime, ancient Memories of the star children.

The residual dust of humanity's past drifts around you. How quickly does it settle! Yes! Very quickly! Slumber not overlong, for the new age soon will be upon you! Memories of dusky nights long forgotten swirl in your souls like clouds of birthing stars. We embrace and enfold you. We tug at your sleeping shoulders as a mother does her cherished babe.

Come Home! Come Home!

We await you here in these ships. We gaze down upon you, you who are as numbly unconscious as four-leaf clovers growing out of grasses. Will you remain silently unresponsive? Simple is the process of awakening, if you but understood it. You must learn to trust, to love, and to accept the essential truth of your soul's eternal beauty.

We urge that you contemplate these last remarks.

You will find about your planet many messages being laid down. Our recordings are like stories told to children, over and over and over again. 'Tis only to perk up your heart's fancies. 'Tis only to tumble and nourish the patterns of your escalating growth as you begin to ascend into realms of celestial perfection. The future glistens like morning's dew inviting flowers to play. We, who are planetary overseers for your spatial system, invite you to freely call upon us and to become as one with us.

Targeted for the enjoyment of those who awaken will be the ability to pluck and harvest blooms of growth that open like roses blushing before the kiss of a summer's shower. We further reiterate: That Which Is Omnipotent Universal Mind is not something to be contemplated as merely a suppositional exercise for philosophical discussion.

Do you believe that your name may have been dropped from the invitation list to visit the stars? We do not pick and choose among you as if we were out gathering daisies! You, sweet-loved one, will come to know us well. Eventually, you will come to understand, and in the grandest fashion. Your ardent, curious questions will be answered. The warmth of the sun's rays and the coolness of the moon's beams equally anticipate the lifting of the fog that has so long hidden your passion behind the sometimes cold, sometimes hot cloudy fluctuations of your basically loving nature.

Such delight never to fall into the need for shelter and all the other things necessary to maintain your bodies in safe, comfortable environments! As the Golden Age evolves and Earth becomes situated in her fifth-dimensional resting place, such trivialities will swiftly disappear. Slumber not along now! The time is short! Be about your star gatherings!

Essay 9

Palpae

Narrow viewpoints are self-serving. Do you suppose that we who dwell in starships remain unaware of the mental images you send skittering into the ethers? It would serve us all if humans would attempt to closely monitor the fractured nature of their busy thoughts.

This is a time for those who are courageous enough to withstand the demands of a judgmental society. Such a society seems bent upon a mode of nonappreciation toward those human channels who are surrendering the illusive privacy of their minds to welcome what they perceive as interdimensional starships.

Earth is coming to terms with the extent of her karmic sacrifice. Throughout time she has allowed a multitude of beings to live upon her frame who rush about from life to life creating karma. Incarnated beings of the Arcturian star system are among those long-slumbering souls who are now awakening. For the most part, they continue to suffer a considerable amount of emotional anguish. As their ancient Memories stir, their heart-minds begin to capture small glimpses of Cheuel, their Arcturian home planet, exploding. In time they will recall the part they themselves played in her demise. Like a jewel was green Cheuel, and the memory of her beauty lives like an aching torch in the hearts of those souls who resided upon her at the time of the great tragedy. Not unlike Earth was her sister planet, Cheuel. The imagery of her once-majestic vistas are duplicated in such places as the Yellowstone of the spirit gods, the ripe lush gardens of the Amazon, and the slow meandering rivers of India. Five million years now gone did Cheuel meet her untimely death.

Essay 10

Palpae

The future's challenges are palpably tangible. Those starseeds who are awakening are subtly extricating themselves from the restrictions, confinements, and situational limitations that third-dimensional entities normally experience as life. Intuitively (though not fully aware) they are beginning to reach out somewhat awkwardly with etheric fingers to playfully and delightfully grasp the gossamer threads that link the strings of human destiny inexorably with those of the dawning golden era.

There has never been a time when war and poverty were not known within your world. In the next century the energy of these things, which has been so burdensome to your species, will completely dissipate. The day is not far ahead when the many nations will announce to the world, "Yes, we *are* one people." On that day carnage and slaughter will cease, and even the pain of dis-ease will lessen. That day will herald a great moment, the day humanity attains full species' maturity. As one world united, humanity's duly appointed representatives will become eligible to sit in Oneness with beings of light serving upon the multigalactic star councils.

Like magpies, our incessant chatterings flutter about you. We present you with much to do, for we are poised to welcome you among our own. Quite profoundly, we reiterate for your pleasure that the plans from which the star nation operates have the name "Earth beings" engraved upon them.

Believe in what is written in conjunction with our many Earth scribes. Observe, as well, the images that from time to time flicker briefly bright in the corners of your eyes. Our forms are like incandescent flames that gleefully dance at the extreme limits of your peripheral vision.

There are many whose hunger for spiritual nutrients grows stronger than their physical requirements for daily nourishment. Internally, the lights of these beautiful beings have begun to unfold like petals of a newly blooming flower. About the essences of you who constantly invoke God's Will angels dance. Celestial trumpets ring loud and clear as subtle notes announce to the spiritually attentive that the long-awaited day is near. Soon, The Christ Essence will descend from the clouds. Fully resplendent in His glorious raiment, He will shine like a newly born sun.

Though you may perceive the messages contained within this manuscript as being somewhat astonishing, we believe that their content is not unduly frightening. It is the intention behind these writings to entice everyone to seek enlightenment.

We resonate with cosmic force, with Light-Love. From That Which Is Ever Present our activities are thus directed. From the Star Maker to the star riders all is clearly perceived and all is understood. Will you not join us? Our beings desire your presence among us. Join us, play with us! Our joyous laughter rings from star to star. We Are! We Are! Come *be* with us as One.

Hear me, Earth people. It will indeed be unfortunate if the urgent needs of Earth Mother must be met through the techniques of painful surgery, for like a cancer unchecked your iniquities have spread throughout her vital organs. You must surely realize that dark cells of environmental pollutants cannot be sustained within her cellular membranes for long. Must you continuously swarm and argue among yourselves as if you were nothing more than a teeming army of ants consuming beetles?

All-inclusive perfection is surely not what is requested of you, but certainly good, solid individual and collective intent to right what is morbidly dis-eased is required. The situation, as it now stands, requires a great deal more effort. However, do not allow the dismay of overreaction to fall upon you as you hark to the difficulties presented. Remember, the words of this manuscript also stress your inherent, essential beauty. We strongly remind you: You are not a dingy sock tucked into a dirty shoe, hidden behind a pant leg! You are potential light, the mystery of ancient times come forth. Your inner Self is like a tinkling silver-hued crystal bell. Like the day's sun, rise high and shine forth your brilliant light upon the horizon's purpled hills. You are like songs sparrows sing from the swaying branches of summer-dressed trees. Wake up! Wake up! It is not necessary to belittle yourselves or others with self-defeating admonitions.

There are many things that you, as a species, have yet to learn. That which faces you in the coming years will prove to be greatly demanding, but you *will* emerge with much practical growth accomplished.

As a member of the Arcturian councils, it is my position to serve as an intergalactic coordinator for contractual distribution affairs in cooperative agreement with the Government of One, as it comes into being upon planet Earth. You will see a day when I speak through the wires of your communication transmitters. In complete harmony, humans and beings of light will easily understand one another. You will come to recognize me as a personality not unlike that of your closest companions. I, Palpae of Arcturus, am as One Entity with you. That I am. So be you and I the same!

Chapter 11

On Pyramids, Vortices, and Grids

QUAKER

Listen carefully, beings! Recorded messages laid throughout time within various structures upon planet Earth are essentially useful for pinpointing telepathic alignments from your solar system to the Pleiades. Embedded within the core of your planet are atomiclike regenerating fuel-source materials that offset debilitating energies of those who are not willing to answer the call to evolution—that is, the sleeping ones.

My essence is in harmonic rhapsody with the sweet tones of your system's farthermost planet, from which transmissions flung out by Earth and her moon are relayed to the crystalline giants situated upon the planets of the Pleiadian star system.

Essay 1

Pyramids are receptors and transmitters of ethereal light. When starships focus light rays upon a third-dimensional pyramid (Pyramid of Giza, for example), the light is instantly transformed into information. Though not physically observable, data thus deposited are stored within crystalline chambers deep inside the pyramid where the unenlightened cannot meddle with or destroy precious recordings but where the awakening may retrieve answers.

Pyramids, however, may best be viewed as conceptual markers for receiving and transmitting telepathic thought. The cap of the pyramid is the focal point. Gently rising from its massive base, the pyramid's pinnacle stands like an observation sentinel. The apex is optimally conducive to fine-tune beacons of colored lights that constantly ply to and fro from "computerized" crystalline recording devices maintained, perpetually humming, upon the starships.

In ancient times, star travelers erected many pyramidal shapes upon Earth. Though many pyramids are obviously land based, many etheric, fourth-dimensional pyramids (which are also storage containers) lie buried within the seas, within certain mountain ranges, and beneath important artifacts. Examples are the remarkable pyramids placed beneath the grid connectors—"landing strips"—and pictographs of the Nazca Plains on the

Peruvian coastal plains. Crystalline pyramids are secreted beneath each of the gigantic land pictures of the arid Nazca regions; the designs symbolically silhouette the data contained within. The capped points of the buried pyramids are kept in perfect alignment with the resonating hum of the star system that corresponds most exactly with the information the pyramid contains. The outline of each gargantuan figure, as drawn in ancient times, was a cooperative effort between indigenous people and representatives of the star councils.

Additionally, there are critically important crystalline-formed fourth-dimensional (astral level) pyramids within mountain ranges throughout the world. Volcanoes such as Mount Shasta and magnificent sacred mountain ranges such as the Himalayas in Asia, Ayers Rock in Australia, and the Tetons in the western United States house important etheric pyramids.

Essay 2

Dotting Earth are innumerable whirling, polarized energy fields called vortices. Intuitive natives, shamans in particular, so thoroughly understood the application of vortex energies that they were capable of embedding Earth's natural powers into items they used daily as well as into shields warriors carried into battle. These shields served as miniature force fields. Properly prepared, they were small, potent bundles of swirling energies that quite effectively connected their owners to corresponding vortices in the ground or sky.

Planetary vortices are created wherever two etheric grids intersect. These grids are strips of pulsating light, essential base material from which planets are formed. Grids (also known as strands or ley lines) and their interweaving vortices are all made up of components of Light-Love that hum as Aum or Ohm—Universal Intelligence. The grids interweave and dance with the most delicious of aromas, as if each were the sweetest, most delicate of flowers. Overlaying and crisscrossing one another, the grids and vortices form a gridlike design.

The grids function like so much cosmic glue, bonding the atoms of physical matter into stars and planets and aligning the melodies of the celestial song into the dimensional octave appropriate to the vibrational hum of each universe. The physics of a planetary system, such as gravity and other solar phenomena, has its root elements solidly entrenched in the gridlike structures of the strands.

Many ancient cultures intuitively recognized the powerful energies running throughout Earth's body. Select individuals within each tribe were trained to pinpoint forces that constantly emanate from the intersecting regions of Earth grids. Stonehenge in England is an excellent example of a resourceful people using the ground-gripping webs to create a structure so powerful that, for several centuries, it served priestly initiates as a stargate.

For the time being, cosmic-oriented, spiritually based physics will continue to be unacceptable to practitioners of logic-linear, intellect-oriented physical and biological sciences. Be that as it may, because the energy draw of a major vortex is so intense, the builders of cathedrals, churches, temples, and so forth often unwittingly erect them upon sites directly overlaying one of the pulsating, intersecting webs.

Drifting dreamily through space, grids serve as a massive celestial connecting system, binding planets to suns, linking suns to suns and galaxies to galaxies. Although each planet and each sun are affixed to the vibrational ratio of a particular dimensional octave, each hums its individual hum in splendid harmony with the whole—Creation's magnificent, eternal song.

ESSAY 3

Rooted in the etheric, gridlines (or grids) are constructions of interwoven, translucent, weblike patterns of purified light. Fashioned from high-magnitude Love energy, light essence is a cohesive binder that holds celestial bodies in physical form. Planetary gridlines surround and, in a sense, swallow Earth in undulating, high-voltage energy waves. Delicately structured light grids readily absorb positive and negative energy radiations basic to human thought emissions. Thus, they are easily affected by fluctuating interplays exuding as electrically charged neurons that constantly pulsate from the average human brain. Fortunately, steadier, more predictable thoughts arise from mind energies of free-playing animal and plant creatures, which tends to harmonize the imbalance created by humanity's more erratic transmissions.

That which transpires in the ethereal is much more critical than humans are wont to suppose. Unbeknownst to the majority, humankind has always been, more or less, a willing participant in what may accurately be likened to cosmic games. Members of the human race have traditionally assumed their favored position of pitting the wits and emotions of the home team in direct opposition to the "meddling" forces of the "visiting" team. Nevertheless, as our turn comes to carry the ball, we hurriedly realign critically disruptive configurations arising in the planetary grids. Motivated by the dynamics of its conflict-worshiping cultural heritage, the habitually agitated, emotional-response-oriented human populace is relatively quick to throw the ball back into the opposite court.

We will be very pleased when our earthbound cousins challenge themselves to awaken in sufficient numbers to actively disperse the disruptive harmonics of negative thought waves for those more conducive to peaceful interaction with forces who represent the interests of Love-Light. In no other way will humans lay aside their burdens and begin gravitating toward responsible team play with the intergalactic league. The ability of humans to transpose negative thought to positive (that is, Love-Light) will ultimately decide their place in the cosmos, and the final score of this most critical, celestial game will be settled.

Temporarily, we will be placing *Marigold—City of Lights* into circular orbit high above Earth. Positioning ourselves to travel around her circumference, we will lace her delicate etheric grids with tonal layers of both flute-like and harplike vibratos. As *Marigold*'s magnificent form passes through layers of the world's auric body, the reverberations exuding through her wake will be most refined in harmonic qualities. As her crystalline "engines" subtly move us forward, her delicate song will be heard worldwide by awakening, telepathic, finely tuned humans. Enraptured by her song, those whose hearts and intuitive minds are open will stand still for a moment, as if becoming temporarily transfixed. From this day forth, those who listen closely will hear the stars singing, calling to them, "Walk closely with God! Come Home! Come Home!"

Marigold's round-the-planet journey will be brief, and then, once again, she will settle her vast, glorious bulk into a more-or-less-fixed position high above the radiant lands of the Northern Hemisphere.

Be aware that we who travel freely upon the space grids are made up of energy patterns like those within your bodies. Primarily, we are beings who sparkle like bits of gleaming fire. Our bodies are microcosmic essences of That Which Shines as Resplendent Light. Our harmonics are in vibrational accord with tones hummed by the planets of our home suns.

Listen, my friends, for the song Earth Mother hums. So very sweetly does she sing. Be aware that the vibrational tones of her unique personality are her cosmic identification "tag." Know also that her resonations are most familiar to great multitudes of beings whose resident suns are placed elsewhere throughout the vastness of this galaxy.

ESSAY 4

Learned ones, be advised that important archaeological sites lay atop certain highly charged grid structures within the greater Pacific and mid-Atlantic regions. These are remains of civilizations whose memories are embedded deep within the psyches of a majority of the world's populace. Though the existence of Lemuria (Mu, the Mother Land) and Atlantis are vehemently dismissed by the scientific elite as unsubstantiated nonsense, the day rapidly approaches when a small handful of "intellectually privileged" will inadvertently stumble upon artifacts buried deep within the seas, the existence of which they will not find easy to explain. Suddenly, distinguished scholars will make world-shaking "discoveries" of ancient, hauntingly familiar civilizations.

Because of the narrow mental and emotional confines of cosmically closed-off humanity, the masses are currently unable to absorb star-link information in an open and agreeable fashion, no matter how carefully writings are set down. Thus, at this juncture the teachings are mainly used as tools for transformative enlightenment by the spiritually adventurous. Nevertheless, humanity is rapidly nearing a time when the majority will find themselves more or less forced to come to terms with information contained within primers already widely available.

Details and nuances of solar data applicable to all aspects of human life will begin to sit comfortably with even the most stubbornly resistant.

ESSAY 5

Vortices, varying in degrees of size and intensity, are localized spots of heightened energies radiating from key positions on crisscrossing grids. As a point of reference: Overlapping an eight-state western geographic region of the country somewhat euphemistically referred to as the "United" States is a massive whirling vortex we refer to as the western medicine wheel. Just as a whirlpool forms upon an ocean's floor and rises until it breaks the surface, energies within the earth began to spin and increased in size and momentum, emerging from the earth's surface to ascend into the etheric. This vortex is persistently relinquishing Earth's denser vibrations as her tonal resonations continue to refine. Contained within the wheel are many subvortices measuring no more than a few inches to several feet or many miles in diameter. Wheels also spin within wheels within wheels.

Many who live and travel in the wheel's land mass are well aware that certain meditative, Earth-honoring rituals they sometimes feel compelled to perform are critically important in terms of healing and restructuring the grids. If nothing else, these intuitive people are at least subconsciously aware that layers of etherically charged energies are constantly swirling throughout Earth's lands, seas, and skies.

By no means is this vortex unique. Findhorn Gardens in Scotland, mountain ranges and sites held sacred by indigenous populations, the vast Lemurian Triangle (a region more or less encompassed by Easter Island, New Zealand, and the Hawaiian Islands), and the Bermuda Triangle are all excellent examples of critical longitudes and latitudes where grid and vortex energies are particularly acute. Force fields lying within the latter two regions are so significantly charged that they function as portals for interdimensional starship access and as space-warp windows for time travel.

The most active of the vortices are equipped with crystalline "computerized" generators programmed to constantly receive and transmit information carried by beams of colored light that constantly ply between Earth's surface and the starships. Starships are more or less permanently berthed in fixed positions over such planetary "hot spots."

The accelerated nature that light, sound, and scent take within the whirling energies of vortices is most resourceful for "beaming up" the etheric bodies of humans who work in cooperative alliance with the star councils, a procedure not detrimental to their emotional, mental, or physical states. Perhaps an etheric presence has been invited for a council function. At times, highly evolved knowledge may be more easily translated into terms the human mind can grasp when in direct proximity to the crystalline data banks. Perhaps nothing more than a friendly guided tour is planned. Ofttimes, special gatherings and assemblies are held to present awards and bestow distinctions of merit upon those whose lives are dedicated to enhance God's Light upon Earth.

We suggest that you critically regard data that refer to the hum or harmony of the universes, galaxies, suns, planets, moons, and so forth. Sound expressed as Aum or Ohm is prime tonal, a basic ingredient of universal energy; it is the glue that binds Creation in cohesive Oneness. The term "poppy- or rose-scented wisps" refers to scented, flowered coordinates that are the by-products or the bouquets of the harmonics. As elusive as they may be on the physical plane, sound, scent, and light are nevertheless capable of blending together to form a tangible, cosmically adaptable substance visible to fifth- and sixth-dimensional entities.

The structural foundation of planets, moons, and so forth is not so grossly dense as humans tend to believe. Rather, base cosmic building blocks are an amalgamation of materials of ethereal consistency. The attraction that maintains planets in alignment with one another in any solar system is the magnetism that draws them to their system's sun or suns. The responsibility for maintaining a solar family in perpetual balance, as appropriate to a particular system's evolutionary status, is centralized in the supreme trustees of individual systems. For example, the dynamics of your sun-star planetary family are the particular concern of The Christ Essence (Sananda) and the Spiritual Hierarchy. The Intergalactic Brotherhood of

Light is formally assigned and serves as instructed and designated by these trustees.

We, the Arcturians, a subdivision of the Supreme Hierarchical Council for Planetary Ascension, System Sol, have established base operations upon the planet Saturn. Uniquely intertwining with grid vortices that align all Sol's family to the vibrational lights of giant Jupiter's mighty hum, Saturn's unique, revolving crystalline rings are particularly conducive to capturing and containing delicate webs of crisscrossing energies that bind together all the system's planets. Saturn's luminous energies were chosen to serve our diverse requirements as an inter-system starbase.

Critical to Earth's position within the planetary grouping are her unique energies, which are in symphonic agreement with the humming tones of both Jupiter and Saturn. The three form a geometric triad of highly radiant light linking Earth to her sister planets and their moon satellites, in particular those of Mars and Venus. Other triads, quadrads, and quintads intermingle throughout the system's spatial regions, embracing in perpetual, steady Oneness all members of Sol's exotic family.

Each planetary coordinate forms its distinct ray or rays of floating, sweetly scented, multihued singing lights. At grid intersection points, interstellar beams connect celestial energies, binding planet to planet and star to star. A vast, gridlike network of brilliant radiance is created as each sun-star's family is caught in the ecstatic harmonics of the immense interstellar web.

Those in late twentieth-century physics and technology fields do not center their computations upon planetary and multispecies spiritual evolution. The majority have not yet arrived at an intellectual understanding that Love, in the form of base light seeking Prime Light, is foundation-building material for physical manifestation. Additionally, the scientific community uses language pointing only to presumptive, linear-logical, third-dimensional conclusions.

In summary: A grid-point vortex is a self-contained thought-sensitive whirling system of specialized energies made up of strands of constantly spinning, spiraling etheric lights. Sweetly scented, as the essence of a fine perfume, each strand hums in tonal accord with a colored hue peculiar to light fibers of the vortex's uniqueness. A shimmering ball made up of dancing, blushing bands of delicately elasticized cords of radiant light serves as a point of reference from which it is best to visualize the networking web of fused energies making up the gauzy fabric of the celestial grids.

Chapter 12

ON DOLPHINS, PORPOISES, AND WHALES

PALPAE AND TASHABA

All things are connected! There is no separation of matter from galactic quadrant to galactic quadrant. To suppose otherwise is to deny That Which Is. All things are linked as one to Greater Cosmic Mind.

One of the functions of our co-created, "channeled" documents is to generate within your minds a greater receptivity and appreciation for life forms which inhabit Earth with that dangerous creature, human. Along with transformative steps undertaken by awakening people, animals and plants struggle to attain their evolutionary growth in an equal and timely manner.

It is counterproductive to your acceleration if you persist in focusing upon "scientifically" proven constants. For example, the modality that humans experienced as linear time in Earth year 1987 greatly accelerated and continues to undergo exceptional tuning refinements. More aware, "primitive" members of the animal and plant kingdoms retain a higher degree of time cognizance than do humans. The former are much more astute in recognizing the escalating interludes within Mother Earth's base harmonics. In comalike slumber, the latter never do decide to rest. Plants and animals are highly aware of nature's movements. Every cell of their beings resonates with the oceanic tides, with the subtlest of breezes, and with the grunting inhalations and exhalations of Earth as she slides into her appointed slot.

Throughout their span of service to Earth, oceanic mammals have taken it upon themselves to remain in close telepathic contact with beings from the stars, particularly those of their home systems, the Pleiades and the Dog Star, Sirius. Appointed caretakers of the etheric pyramids that function as Earth-ocean energy transfer points to starships, dolphins and whales essentially are frontline maintenance crews for submerged, multispatial, triangular-shaped crystalline monitoring centers.

Throughout history, humankind has been urged by certain cosmically designated animals to assist them in their life's work: that of maintaining gridline harmonics. As an example, in mid-1987 we called upon Manitu and her associates to act with us in a cooperative experiment between land-based humans and their water-based cousins, the dolphins, porpoises, and whales. Like pus accumulating within a giant boil, a massive pocket of accumulated negative energy had been threatening to explode deep within the Pacific substrates. The reserve "fuels" of the crystalline monitoring pyramids anciently set upon the oceanic grids in the Lemurian sector were severely overextended, but they were overwhelmed with positive thought waves forcefully ejected from awakening humans during the Harmonic Convergence Earth Love meditation. Manitu's group in Boise, Idaho, was operating from various stages of confusion because of the rapidity of its members' spiritual awakening; they were somewhat unaware of the ramifications of that in which they were, nevertheless, most willing to participate. But their goodwill and trust toward our mutually shared venture was so true that, at our urgent suggestion, they found the prescribed time to purposefully direct loving thoughts toward the watery deep and to dwell in close mental comradeship with the dolphins, porpoises, and whales. Our human heros bravely merged their thoughts in harmonious mind-meld with their mammalian cousins, thereby relieving what had become overpowering, even to the inestimable abilities of those mammals to successfully hold in unified symmetry without the cooperation of humans.

Though humans who willingly participated in the energy transactions were essentially mountain based, they learned an important lesson as they realized the power of individual thought when merged in agreeable tones with others. This is especially true when many minds, acting as one, focus a concentrated ray of thought upon a predetermined location. When telepathed as Love-Light from the heart's heat core, the light wattage of a spiritually evolving human essentially reaches force-field intensity.

For millennia, though they have been greatly maligned by their human caretakers, plants and animals have borne their planetary chores with much dignity. But because of positive refinement of the whirling grid vortices set in motion in mid-1987, a many-hued aura began to surround Earth's etheric body. The sea, land, and sky creatures resonate much more delightfully now. With the advent of larger numbers of awakening humans, many difficult responsibilities the creatures hold for maintaining the integrity of Earth's grid structures have been completely alleviated in some key areas and lessened in many others. Gratefully, these beings mind-think a most hearty thank-you as they wrap their essences in Oneness with the submissive minds of more subdued, peace-oriented, nature-loving members of the human family. Gridline healing accelerates as awakening individuals willingly gravitate toward service to high purpose.

As you progress along your spiritual path, the light harmonics of your internal energies will steadily purify, degree by degree. Eventually you will become aware of a secure telepathic link with multilevel beings who inhabit Earth.

Much cancerouslike dis-ease remains within the dermal layers of Mother Earth's crusted surface. Her otherwise naturally clean pores have become filthy, clogged by poisonous toxins and pollutants humans are constantly depositing into the folds of her delicate skin and belching forth into her air, sea, and land; by corrosive wastes; and most critically, by nuclear residue that continuously oozes from improperly sealed containers.

Fondest regards from your star brothers to you eager individuals who are purposefully and progressively activating the functioning ability of your higher Selves to manifest Love's Essence as a constant expression of daily life. From the far corners of this majestic world, you who wander are awakening to that which profoundly calls you. As your cellular membranes refreshen, you gallant beings show an innate ability to courageously modify your lives to reflect your rising degree of spiritual integrity. Never before cognizant that it was always yours to perform, you are rapidly becoming adept at using your minds as purposeful instruments for producing and relaying precisely enhanced mental pictures. The art of healing Earth is effectively executed by projecting select, wholesome neural synapse voltage to predetermined geographic points. Using the art of creative imagery and transmitting it for planetary healing is tremendously beneficial in alleviating dangerous negative energies constantly accumulating within the shell-like surface regions of evolutionary-primed Earth. Much relief is obtained within her rocky organs whenever a human mind links in rapturous Oneness with others for the expressed purpose of healing her.

It is important to remember that the marine-based dolphins, porpoises, and whales (whose numbers witless people have decimated) are primary intergalactic agents responsible for maintenance of energy balance within the oceanic grids. They enhance the harmonic tones Earth Mother sings in mutual concordance with Greater Celestial Hum.

Quantra

Ground forces in human form are becoming increasingly adept at multidimensional telepathy. Cosmically cooperative, intuitive, mystically oriented humans are adjusting their daily routines to function within the boundaries suggested by their extrastellar guides. Worldwide, it has become commonplace for many humans to prearrange a date and time for meditating upon a mutually agreed-upon subject.

In times of meditative stillness, the auric, chakra, and light bodies of the spiritually attuned begin transmitting high degrees of electrically charged energy. In peak moments of peaceful internal contemplation or spiritual ecstasy, these beings often radiate subatomic-force voltage power. As they surrender themselves to God's Will, their spirit bodies begin to emanate subtly refined tones.

Quite literally, they begin to function like shortwave radios, simultaneously receiving and sending.

For the most part, most humans are not aware they are actively participating in delicate, Earth-healing procedures. Using the crown chakras of these wondrous beings as miniature targets upon which to focus beams of sweetly humming light, crystalline starships pass multi-hued rays directly through their human energy systems. Such maneuvers cleanse and purify their emotional, mental, and spiritual bodies while ministering to the needs of Earth Mother. The light body of a meditating human acts as an effective anchor to capture, hold, and disseminate high-potency light into dis-at-eased sections within the grids to balance Earth's dangerously stressed areas. The willing, conscious agreement of growing numbers of humans to work in close harmony with the star nations greatly accelerates the tempo of Earth's regenerative procedures.

Starseeds often find themselves drawn to visit or to reside in particular geographic areas. These excursions allow us an opportunity to focus information telepathically through them as we step up our efforts to peacefully contact ever-widening groups of Earth's citizens. Although this may seem manipulative, nevertheless, free will remains intact; it follows only what is, at any rate, the starseed's overriding desire. To the conscious minds of participating humans, it may appear that nothing more important than a pleasant conversation between two or more people is underway. However, if you were to closely observe them from a starship, you would see radiant beams of auric light exuding from the core heat of these humans. If you consider the roles our ground forces play, you will understand that the human energy system greatly facilitates light-exchange work undertaken by starship personnel.

Adonai!

Chapter 13

Summary of the
Initial Seed Messages

The Arcturians

If you desire to evolve interdimensionally, we tell you that spiritual, emotional, mental, and physical integrity and self-discipline are extremely critical. In all enterprises of your life and in all encounters with other life forms, you must double and even triple your efforts to focus upon these things as being of number one priority.

Inwardly visualize the millions of stars making up the Milky Way. Imagine, as best you might, their accompanying planets with their respective lunar satellites. Each brilliant dot in the night sky is a microscopic magnification of God's Goodness, Essence, and Love in physical manifestation. These worlds that are belong to everyone. They are yours and ours to explore.

Earth's gravitational pull greatly hampers free movement of the human form, yet the inquisitive mind, unencumbered by any such limiting constraints, soars uninhibited about the universe. Those of creative bent capably document their mystical interdimensional experiences, expertly capturing on paper and canvas the images of their inward journeys. The covers of science "fiction" and "fantasy" novels—and abstract and surrealistic paintings—are replete with the ripe colors and exquisite forms of the intra- and extrastellar planets. The vibrational humming tones of distant worlds whisper their sweet, haunting strains through the melodic structurings of softly meditative music.

Within this manuscript we have been privileged to communicate with our human brethren on many mutually interesting subjects. We highlight but a few of significant importance.

We urgently suggest that you begin focusing on your latent psychic talents and develop a way to use them in your daily life. Those who persistently practice merging thought interdimensionally will eventually find themselves joined in ecstatic harmonic Oneness with beings of light. As people of Earth become spiritually conscious and planetarily responsible, they will find themselves happily laying aside the trappings of their befuddled infancy.

Equally important is the endeavor to consciously surrender into the arms of Love all of fear's many facets, particularly humanity's greatest fear, the fear of bodily death. To fear death is to fear life itself. Any fear that persistently eats away at your emotional and mental body creates an energy drain upon your physical form, lowers your innate exuberance for life, and invites a host of parasitic diseases to invade your body's cellular matrix. It would serve you well to come to a clear, comprehensive intellectual and emotional understanding that death is not life's finale. Death is nothing more than your spirit extending itself into a new wealth of alternatives and possibilities for the fine-tuning of your soul's holy journey.

Further acknowledge that what is reaped and sown in one life could very well be sown and reaped for many, many lifetimes. Karma—the Law of Cause and Effect— is fundamental to Universal Law. Unconditional, non-judgmental Love for everyone, including yourself, is the fundamental clause that balances Universal Law and Cosmic Justice.

The tenets of Universal Law and Cosmic Justice are grounded on the rocky slopes of free will. The Law of Free Will grants each individual the choice to shine like a brightly lit beacon or to plunge like an avalanche from the peaks of sun-struck mountains into rock-filled canyons.

We warn those who remain innocent of the unsavory side of extraworld doings that not all beings who hail from other star systems have evolved spiritually to attain vibrational status within the higher dimensions. Indeed, among the stellar entities visiting planet Earth during these times of transmutation are small contingents of dis-ruptive beings who remain ensnared in harsh nets cast by the Dark Lords. Originating from vast populations of more agreeable beings, certain rebellious, disharmonious entities from the star systems Orion and Zeta Reticulum (in particular) are much tantalized by humanity's dark side. These intrusive, manipulative beings look for escalating signs of human corruption to promote their unscrupulous deeds. They watch for manifestations that point to growing ethical and moral erosion within the world's governments, megabusinesses, and religious organizations. There is much data available in books, film, and music outlining the less-than-desirable behaviors of these rapacious beings. Become aware of what you give attention to.

If you are resolved to overcome the prickly karmic thorns that torment your spiritual path, continuously observe all your thoughts. Carefully monitor all mental and emotional input and output. Diligently struggle to overcome any focus that stems from or encourages fear-based thought. Remember: Negative thought produces energy waves that project outwardly, manifesting as distress patterns in both the physical and lower astral worlds. Concentrate on evolving the vibrational tones of all judgmental or fear-oriented thoughts. Concentrate on becoming a being who creates only Love's finest vibrations. That which Love's energies emit into the exterior world create, in turn, like vibrations to flow in reverse.

The simplest cosmic rule to remember is that Love's intention manifests Light-Love. Fear's intention manifests darkness and fear.

Seek to harvest the elusive beams of the moon and the rays of colored bows that spill upon Earth when rain and sun embrace. The etheric bodies of those who perpetually strive to duplicate Creation's source energy within their beings sparkle like diamonds of the finest quality light.

Although the ultimate goal is to master spiritual power, vast numbers of highly placed humans have abused the power with which their temporal lives have been entrusted. Thus, many misguided or darkly evil beings have greatly affected the course of history. Individuals who are obsessed with power are often quite rightly viewed as greedy, manipulative, and controlling. In the minds of many, the idea of power as a personal force is laden with frightful, ill-defined, and misunderstood connotations.

On the cosmic level, however, power is potent and vigorous. Its vibrations resonate within the cellular membranes of all living things. When extracted with the highest intent and integrity from the dynamic waves of Universal Intelligence, power is a pure energy source stored as reservoirs of sacred fuel within the spirit bodies of the cosmically dedicated. At some point in their journeys, entities committed to personal and spiritual evolution naturally become adept at manifesting internal and external original-source power (Love as perfected cosmic energy) in all that they think, say, and do.

Planetary maturation activities on Earth rest upon the firm shoulders of the delicate ones, men and women whose lives are devoted to serving Holy Supreme Spirit. These courageous human-bound entities are intent, in this lifetime, to overcome the cycling effects that have bound their essences to Earth for millennia through the Law of Repetition (reincarnation)—the karmic Law of Cosmic Balance. We know these intrepid beings as the sky warriors, the light workers, the eagles of the new dawn.

In the closing years of the twentieth century, humankind is faced with overwhelming problems associated with population explosion, racial and cultural unrest, decaying cities and social institutions, multispecies' extinction, and massive destruction of Earth's environment. It is indeed unfortunate that political, religious, and business leaders whose positions would let them restore inter- and intraspecies peace and environmental health are among those who tumble through life caught in the dark clutches of personal corruption and negativity. Suffering from a chronic condition of morbid short-sightedness, they call themselves privileged but have failed to take into consideration the depth of their responsibility for leading your world into a state of cosmic grace. Otherwise intelligent, they seem almost incapable of coming to grips with the simple fact that nature's fair landscapes abound with the waste and debris of the spiritually ignorant.

As planetary caretakers, every human holds some degree of responsibility for Earth's health. Any being who casts litter or in any manner deliberately degrades or encourages destruction of the natural integrity of the land, sea, or air is karmically accountable for that act. Individuals who do not thoroughly understand that your planet once teemed with multitudes of creatures who are rapidly vanishing because of humanity's self-serving ways cannot even begin to fathom universal prime directives. It is by their doing that many plants and animals are becoming extinct. The lagging human collective has not even begun to come to terms with the mounting dilemma of industrial poisons and inappropriate use of planetary resources. In your heart, can you honestly condone the atrocities that humans continue to perpetuate upon Earth's natural elegance?

Surely we preach! We are not unaware that our advice is often harshly viewed and that the problems you face will not be easily overcome. Nevertheless, there remains much to be done and an extremely short time frame left in which to accomplish it—many long hours in the cosmic classroom, lessons, and tests to be passed before the majority are eligible for graduation into the perpetually peaceful realms. We urge spiritual evolution as a goal worth pursuing. When it is achieved, you will find ecstatic harmonious soul more blessedly wonderful than you have ever imagined.

The Arcturians represent one pure-thought energy form. Relaying as a cooperative unit, we endeavor to select and transmit stimulating words that will encourage emotions of love and hope to swell within your hearts. We realize that at times it appears we address you as if we were overly cautious parents reprimanding wayward children. Nevertheless, for the time being we will retain this communicative style, for we are cognizant of the precarious traps waiting to ensnare the spiritually unwary. Beloved family, to us you are like babes innocently exploring a fascinating new world, a world replete with perilous pitfalls and dangerous temptations.

The verbal streams emanating from this manuscript are meant to challenge you, to draw your wholehearted attention to extremely important matters. The essays are designed to outline all preliminary tasks and interstellar contractual agreements that, as completed, will see humans joining in peaceful Oneness with beings of the greater galactic community. Additionally, this primer outlines, as simply as possible, reasons for gathering a vast intergalactic armada within your solar system and Earth's energy fields. It also impresses upon you that, although we constantly monitor all humans, we interact with individuals only as invited or as spiritually appropriate.

Those whose telepathic tones are presented throughout these essays are fifth- and sixth-dimensional light-formed entities. Because Patricia's base vibrational resonation is in agreement with the hum of the great Arcturian sun, she primarily interacts with like-vibrating entities. Her galactic tutors are the Arcturian star system Intergalactic Brotherhood of Light personnel who receive their directives from Earth coordinate Supreme Commander, The Christ Essence, The Holy One, Sananda.

Fifth- and sixth-dimensional beings act only in

accordance with Universal Law. As such they do not tamper with individual or collective will unless requested to do so—except in situations threatening the stability of Earth. We strongly advise that there are other beings who operate under their own sets of devilish rules. Be aware of these entities and of their intrusive and dangerous ways. Although it is not the place of a spiritually awakening individual to sit in judgment of another being's motives, it is imperative to the safety of the spiritually budding to recognize all multidimensional, negative-oriented energies and to master the simple tools of psychic protection [see Glossary]. Strive to achieve a state of constant awareness. Honestly and critically observe all points of energy reference that arise within your mental, emotional, and physical bodies.

Generations of cosmically ignorant, fear-laden people have succumbed to the powerful manipulations of the Dark Lords. Exploitive, controlling, and abusive, they have enjoyed perpetual access to the potent vibrational by-products that exude from the energies of the collective unconscious. Unaware of such peril, you go about the busy-ness of your lives virtually oblivious to the fact that you are participants in a great cosmic struggle.

Individuals stand, poised like fledgling eaglets, upon the steep cliffs of a rocky precipice. The spiritually attuned are steadily perched, their laser-bright bodies made ready. Soon, these indomitable beings will bravely unfold their cosmic wings and find themselves effortlessly gliding onto the lush fields of a purified world.

Conversely, those humans whose energies are spent in honoring the forces of darkness will find themselves tumbling down a long, shadowy, tunnel-like corridor and emerging onto the ravaged contours of a primal-state planet.

Throughout these pages we have endeavored to set clearly forth the nature of extraworld activities. We have outlined as explicitly as possible (within the limited framework of your language) the unprecedented opportunities associated with spiritual and planetary evolution.

As you come across these pages, and as you freely desire, we invite you to consciously establish telepathic communicative linkup with us. Remember always: Of your being's essence we are most aware. We are aware!

Glossary

ASCENDED MASTERS: Earth-incarnated souls who have overcome death, have assumed their bodies of light, and have attained God-realized Christ Consciousness.

ASTRAL PLANES: Fourth dimension, planes of instant manifestation. The astral is where reincarnating souls attached to Earth dwell between lives. The astral planes are vast and multilayered. The lower astral is where negative beings and negative thought forms reside. The region referred to in religious texts as heaven is the upper astral. See *Octave*.

AUM, OHM: Prime tone, a basic ingredient of universal energy. See *Hum*.

BLUE CRYSTAL PLANET: Closest English translation for the principal light-bodied planet of the Arcturian star system. Primary planning and gathering planet for the multiuniversal, multidimensional star councils.

CELESTIAL HOME: Also referred to as Central Sun. The Soul yearns to return to Celestial Home. It is the Soul's journey's end.

CELLULAR MATRICES: The molecular makeup of all third-dimensional physical matter. Used to describe the human body as well as Earth's body.

CHEUEL: An Arcturian sister planet to Earth destroyed by her citizens because of improper nuclear energy use about five million years ago (in Earth historical time). Abundantly forested and populated with many animals and plants, it was recently restored by the Intergalactic Brotherhood to pristine form. It awaits Arcturian starseeds as a rest and recuperation planet after their mission on Earth is completed.

CHEUEL STARSEEDS: Arcturian starseeds associated with the explosion of Cheuel and the karmic implications of same. Many were implanted upon Earth as long as five million years ago. Their heart-mind (or Soul) Memories retain the vision of Cheuel's destruction. They are programmed to awaken in the latter years of the twentieth century to assist in the evolution of humanity at a critical, parallel time in Earth's evolution.

DARK LORDS: Evil, manipulative, controlling beings who throughout history have attempted to hold humanity in their clutches. They are referred to as satanic beings, Lucifer, and the dark angels. See *Grays*.

DENSITY OCTAVE, DIMENSIONAL OCTAVE: See *Octave*.

EAGLES OF THE NEW DAWN: See *Sky warriors*.

ENERGY FIELDS: Energy fields range from subtle to forcefield magnitude. The energy field that surrounds the human body is the aura. See *Grids* and *Vortex*.

ETHERIC GRID STRANDS: See *Grids*.

FIFTH DIMENSION: Dimension of refined light. Arcturians are fifth- and sixth-dimensional beings. Negative beings are unable to penetrate into the realms of light substance.

FOURTH DIMENSION: See *Astral planes*.

GOD-REALIZED: An enlightened, evolved individual who has attained Christ Consciousness. Spiritual masters are God-realized.

GRAYS: Manipulative extraterrestrials who are in alliance with the Dark Lords. The Grays are responsible for human abductions and cattle mutilations. See *Dark Lords*. See *Hidden Mysteries* by J. D. Stone and *UFOs and the Nature of Reality* by J. P. Koteen for more detailed information.

GRIDS, GRIDLINES, SPACE GRIDS, STAR GRIDS, STRANDS: Crisscrossing webs of light, sound, color, and scent that make up Earth's spiritual body. Starships also travel upon grids of light that weave through space. Grids of light connect galaxy to galaxy, star to star, planet to planet, moon to moon, and so forth. See *Ley lines*. Refer to Part III for more detailed information.

HARMONIC COORDINATES OF THE GALACTIC HUM: The sound coordinates of the grids. See *Hum.*

HEART-MIND: The intuitive, spiritual mind. The heart chakra is the location of the heart-mind. It is where we connect with our higher Selves and our Soul Memories.

HUM: Cosmic creative vibration, the prime or God energy expressed as Aum (Amen) or Ohm. Matter's tonal qualities. Pythagoras described hum as the music of the spheres.

INTERGALACTIC BROTHERHOOD OF LIGHT: Spiritually evolved, light-formed, fifth- and sixth-dimensional extraterrestrials from many star systems and many universes. See *Spiritual Hierarchy* and *Star councils.*

LANGUAGE OF THE SUN: Common mode of telepathic communication natural to all beings. Also called solar tongue or solar language.

LEY LINES: Grids associated with the stone monuments of England (Stonehenge, for example) and the European continent.

LIGHT-LOVE OR LOVE-LIGHT: Light is the first manifestation of God in form; Love is God's Essence or energy. Light-Love incorporates Creation's energy as a physical manifestation. Sound (vibration) is integral to Light-Love energy. Throughout the ages Earth's God-realized spiritual masters have referred to Light-Love as Universal Love.

LIGHT STRANDS: See *Grids*.

LORDS OF DARKNESS: See *Dark Lords*.

LOVE AND love: Unconditional Love is integrated Cosmic Intelligence. However, love is the emotion humans feel for others, their pets, and Earth.

MANITU: Meaning "spirit keeper," it is the title the Intergalactic Brotherhood bestows on people whose life's purpose is planetary healing.

MARIGOLD—CITY OF LIGHTS: Intergalactic Brotherhood Earth-based mother ship. Authors may refer to it by other names, perhaps *City of Lights, Jeweled City, Crystal City, New Jerusalem.* The term *Marigold* was given to this writer as a symbolic clue that cosmic light incorporates vibration, color, and scent. The mother ship in the movie *Close Encounters of the Third Kind* portrays her essence, though *Marigold–City of Lights* is much larger.

MEMORIES: Aspect of Self-knowledge slumbering humanity has forgotten; Soul Memories. As we awaken to our spiritual nature, the Memories are reactivated.

OCTAVE: A dimensional or density span. The vibrational layers within a dimension are not unlike the notes of the musical scale, ever softening in an upward or refining manner.

PSYCHIC PROTECTION: The purposeful use of Light-Love when meditating or channeling. The following steps are recommended: cleansing one's physical environment with incense or sacred herbs (smudging); requesting Christ Consciousness energy (see *Spiritual Hierarchy*) to assist; visualizing light running through the chakras and surrounding the body in an energy bubble; using a repetitive, vibrational tone or mantra (for example, Aum or Ohm); and routinely forcefully challenging any entity with the statement "Are you of the Light (spiritual beings)?" (See Part II, "Patricia Meets Palpae.") Beings of light expect to be challenged. Negative beings cannot penetrate the layers of a Light-Love established force field.

POPPY- OR ROSE-SCENTED WISPS: Refers to scented, flowered coordinates that are the by-products or the bouquets of the harmonics. The Arcturians find the symbolic use of flowers helpful in explaining the fragrant qualities of the light grids.

RESONANT VIBRATIONAL HUM: Degree of refined light vibrating within a dimensional octave.

SIXTH DIMENSION: See *Fifth dimension*.

SKY WARRIORS: Awakened humans (and animals) who interact with the star councils for the purpose of serving humanity's evolution. Also called the eagles of the new dawn.

SPACE GRIDS: See *Grids*.

SPIRITUAL HIERARCHY: Body of One, supreme spiritual council in service to Earth's ascension. The central figure is The Christ Essence. The council includes archangels and angelic realms, ascended masters, the brotherhoods of light (including the Intergalactic Brotherhood of Light), and God-realized humans. See *Book of Knowledge, Keys of Enoch* by J. J. Hurtak for more detailed information on the brotherhoods of light.

STAR COUNCILS: Coordinators and directors of multi-spatial, intergalactic business affairs. All aware galactic citizens have input upon the star councils. Arcturians in service to Earth sit upon the star councils as a subdivision of the Supreme Hierarchical Council for Planetary Ascension, System Sol, Intergalactic Brotherhood of Light.

STAR GRIDS: See *Grids*.

STARGATE: A multidimensional access window. See the movies *2001: A Space Odyssey* and *Stargate* for a graphic portrayal of stargate dynamics.

STARSEEDS: Galactic beings on Earth as humans, animals, and plants. Many universes and star systems are represented, among them Arcturus, Pleiades, Sirius, and Orion.

STRANDS: See *Grids*.

VORTEX: Varying degrees of heightened energies that arise from a point along a grid where light strands crisscross. Vibration and light energy arising from a vortex varies greatly and may range from a few inches to miles. Intuitively, humans have always recognized vortices as power spots or sacred sites. Refer to Part III for more detailed information.

WISPS: See *Poppy- or rose-scented wisps.*

YIN-YANG: Ancient Chinese symbol used in the teachings of the Tao and the I Ching. Yin is feminine; yang is masculine. Yin-yang demonstrates all polarities and diversities (the ten thousand things) that exist within the universal whole.

232

Suggested Books and Movies

Books

Agartha, Journey to the Stars. M. L. Young. Stillpoint, 1984.

Aliens Among Us. R. Montgomery. New York: Fawcett-Crest, 1985.

Ancient America, Great Ages of Man. (Nazca Lines.) New York: Time-Life Books, 1967.

Autobiography of a Yogi. P. Yogananda. Los Angeles: Self-Realization Fellowship, 1946.

Bashar, Blueprint for Change. D. Anka. Seattle: New Solutions, 1990.

Beyond Stonehenge. G. Hawkins. (Nazca Lines.) New York: Harper & Row, 1973.

Book of Knowledge, Keys of Enoch. J. J. Hurtak. Los Gatos, Calif.: Academy for Future Science, 1977.

Bringers of the Dawn. B. Marciniak. Santa Fe, N.M.: Bear, 1992.

Celestial Raise. (Anthology.) Mt. Shasta, Calif.: ASSK, 1986.

Crystal Stair. E. Klein. Livermore, Calif.: Oughten House, 1990.

Divine Romance. P. Yogananda. Los Angeles: Self-Realization Fellowship, 1986.

Earth Chronicles, Vols. I–V (and other works). Z. Sitchin. New York and Sante Fe, N.M.: Avon and Bear, 1980–1993.

Earth's Birth Changes. (St. Germain through Azena.) Cairns, Q.N.S., Australia: Triad.

ET 101, Cosmic Instruction Manual. Z. Joh. San Francisco: Harper Collins, 1990.

Findhorn Garden. Findhorn Community. Harper & Row, 1975.

God I Am. P. Erbe. Cairns, Q.N.S., Australia: Triad.

Gods of Eden. W. Bramley. New York: Avon Books, 1989.

Hidden Mysteries, ETs, Ancient Mystery Schools, and Ascension. J. D. Stone. Sedona, Ariz.: Light Tech, 1995.

Kryon, Alchemy of the Human Spirit. L. Carroll. Del Mar, Calif.: Kryon Writings, 1995.

Kryon, Don't Think Like a Human. L. Carroll. Del Mar, Calif.: Kryon Writings, 1994.

Kryon, The End Times. L. Carroll. Del Mar, Calif.: Kryon Writings, 1992.

Lazaris books, videos, and cassettes. Palm Beach, Fla.: Visionary Publishing.

Life and Teachings of the Masters of the Far East,
Vols. I–V. B. T. Spalding. Marina del Rey, Calif.:
Devorss, 1924.

Mary's Message to the World. A. Kirkwood: Putnam,
1991.

Mayan Factor, Path Beyond Technology. J. Arguelles.
Santa Fe, N.M.: Bear, 1987.

Monuments of Mars (book and video). R. C. Hoagland.
North Atlantic Books, 1988.

Nature of Personal Reality (and other Seth books).
J. Roberts. San Rafael, Calif.: Amber-Allen and
New World Library, 1974.

Nothing in This Book Is True. Frissell. Berkeley, Calif.:
North Atlantic, 1993.

Only Planet of Choice. Schlemmer & Jenkins. Bath,
U.K., and United States: Gateway Books and
Atrium, 1993.

Pleiadian Agenda. B. H. Clow. Santa Fe, N.M.: Bear,
1995.

Project World Evacuation. Tuella and the Ashtar
Command. Inner Light Publications.

P'Taah Tapes, An Act of Faith. J. King. Cairns, Q.N.S.,
Australia: Triad, 1991.

Ramtha. J. Z. Knight. Orcas Island, Wash.: Sovereignty,
1986.

Star-Borne, Remembrance for the Awakened Ones.
Solara. Star-Borne, 1989.

Starseed Transmission. K. Carey. San Francisco: Harper
Collins, 1985.

Surfers of the Zuvuya. J. Arguelles. Santa Fe, N.M.: Bear, 1988.

The Third Millennium. K. Carey. San Francisco: Harper Collins, 1991.

Transformation of the Species. J. King. Cairns, Q.N.S., Australia: Triad.

Treasure of El Dorado. J. Whitfield. Treasure, 1989.

UFOs and the Nature of Reality. J. P. Koteen. Eastsound, Wash.: Indelible Ink, 1991.

Vision. K. Carey. San Francisco: Harper Collins, 1982.

We the Arcturians. N. J. Milanovich. Albuquerque, N.M.: Athena, 1990.

With Wings of Eagles. J. R. Price. Quartus Foundation, 1987.

You Are Becoming a Galactic Human. Nidle & Essene. Santa Clara, Calif.: Spiritual Education Endeavors, 1994.

MOVIES ("MANAGEMENT TRAINING FILMS")

2001: A Space Odyssey. Stanley Kubrick film.

2010: The Year We Make Contact. Peter Hyams film.

Always. Steven Spielberg film.

Batteries Not Included. Steven Spielberg film.

Close Encounters of the Third Kind (extended version). Steven Spielberg film.

Cocoon. Ron Howard film.

Defending Your Life. Geffen Pictures.

Field of Dreams. P. A. Robinson film.

Ghost. Jerry Zucker film.

Heart & Souls. Ron Underwood film.

Heaven Can Wait. Paramount.

Hoagland's Mars. Richard C. Hoagland.

Made in Heaven. Lorimar Motion Pictures.

Star Trek, entire series, both motion pictures and television, especially *Star Trek IV, The Voyage Home*.

Star Wars trilogy: *Star Wars, The Empire Strikes Back, Return of the Jedi*. George Lucas film.

Starman. John Carpenter film.

Willow. Ron Howard film.

*Other Books from
Beyond Words Publishing, Inc.*

─────────────

The Book of Goddesses
*Author/illustrator: Kris Waldherr; Introduction: Linda
Schierse Leonard, Ph.D., $17.95 hardcover*
    This beautifully illustrated book introduces readers of
all ages to twenty-six goddesses and heroines from cultures around the world. In the descriptions of these
archetypal women, the author weaves a picture of the
beauty, individuality, and unique strength which are
the birthright of every girl and woman. Beautiful to look
at and inspiring to read, this book is a stunning gift for
goddess-lovers of all ages.

Know Your Truth, Speak Your Truth, Live Your Truth
Author: Eileen R. Hannegan, $12.95 softcover
    To be truly yourself, you need to have an authentic
integration of the mental, emotional, physical, and spiritual truths of self. This book offers a simplified formula of
the ancient truths that escort an individual into personal
and spiritual wholeness. The three-part program assists
individuals in discovering the truth of who they truly are
and thereby in living a more authentic life.

The Woman's Book of Creativity
Author: C Diane Ealy, $12.95 softcover

Creativity works differently in women and men, and women are most creative when they tap into the process that is unique to their own nature—a holistic, "spiraling" approach. The book is a self-help manual, both inspirational and practical, for igniting female creative fire. Ealy encourages women to acknowledge their own creativity, often in achievements they take for granted. She also gives a wealth of suggestions and exercises to enable women to recognize their own creative power and to access it consistently and effectively. Ealy holds a doctorate in behavioral science and consults with individuals and corporations on creativity.

You Can Have It All
Author: Arnold M. Patent, $16.95 hardcover

Joy, peace, abundance—these gifts of the Universe are available to each of us whenever we choose to play the real game of life: the game of mutual support. *You Can Have It All* is a guidebook that shows us how to move beyond our beliefs in struggle and shortage, open our hearts, and enjoy a life of true ecstasy. Arnold Patent first self-published *You Can Have It All* in 1984, and it became a classic with over 200,000 copies in print. This revised and expanded edition reflects his greater understanding of the principles and offers practical suggestions as well as simple exercises for improving the quality of our lives.

Nurturing Spirituality in Children
Author: Peggy D. Jenkins, $10.95 softcover

Children who develop a healthy balance of mind and spirit enter adulthood with higher self-esteem, better able to respond to life's challenges. This book offers scores of simple and thought-provoking lessons that parents can teach to their children in less than ten minutes at a time. Using items easily found around the house, each lesson provides a valuable message for children to take into their days and into their lives. The lessons are easy to prepare and understand, and each parent can alter the lessons to fit their own spiritual beliefs. The activities are adaptable for children from preschool to high school ages.

Letters from the Light: An Afterlife Journal
from the Self-Lighted World
Author: Elsa Barker; Editor: Kathy Hart,
$12.95 hardcover

In the early part of this century, a woman begins a process of "automatic writing." It is as though someone takes over her hand and writes the document. Days later she finds out that the man has died thousands of miles away, and she is now serving as a conduit as he tells of life after death through her. His message: There is nothing to fear in death, and the life after this one is similar in many ways to the one we already know, even though we will be much more able to recognize our freedom. Readers of the book, originally published in 1914, invariably concur that the book removed from them the fear of dying.

**Home Sweeter Home: Creating a Haven of Simplicity
and Spirit**
*Author: Jann Mitchell; Foreword: Jack Canfield,
$12.95 softcover*

We search the world for spirituality and peace—only to discover that happiness and satisfaction are not found "out there" in the world but right here in our houses and in our hearts. Award-winning journalist and author Jann Mitchell offers creative insights and suggestions for making our home life more nurturing, spiritual, and rewarding for ourselves, our families, and our friends.

To order or to request a catalog, contact
Beyond Words Publishing, Inc.
4443 NE Airport Road
Hillsboro, OR 97124-6074
503-693-8700 or 1-800-284-9673

Beyond Words Publishing, Inc.

OUR CORPORATE MISSION:
Inspire to Integrity

OUR DECLARED VALUES:
We give to all of life as life has given us.
We honor all relationships.
Trust and stewardship are integral to fulfilling dreams.
Collaboration is essential to create miracles.
Creativity and aesthetics nourish the soul.
Unlimited thinking is fundamental.
Living your passion is vital.
Joy and humor open our hearts to growth.
It is important to remind ourselves of love.